Seaside

Discover the best of Britain's beaches

Published by Time Out Guides Ltd, a wholly owned subsidiary of Time Out Group Ltd.
Time Out and the Time Out logo are trademarks of Time Out Group Ltd.

© **Time Out Group Ltd 2008**

10 9 8 7 6 5 4 3 2 1

This edition first published in Great Britain in 2008 by Ebury Publishing
A Random House Group Company
20 Vauxhall Bridge Road, London SW1V 2SA

Random House Australia Pty Limited 20 Alfred Street, Milsons Point, Sydney,
New South Wales 2061, Australia
Random House New Zealand Limited 18 Poland Road, Glenfield, Auckland 10,
New Zealand
Random House South Africa (Pty) Limited Isle of Houghton, Corner Boundary Road
& Carse O'Gowrie, Houghton 2198, South Africa

Random House UK Limited Reg. No. 954009

For further distribution details, see www.timeout.com

ISBN 978-1-84670-079-8

A CIP catalogue record for this book is available from the British Library

Printed and bound in Singapore by Tien Wah Press Ltd

The Random House Group Limited supports the Forest Stewardship Council (FSC), the leading
international forest certification organisation. All our titles that are printed on Greenpeace-approved
FSC certified paper carry the FSC logo. Our paper procurement policy can be found at
www.rbooks.co.uk/environment.

Time Out Guides Limited
Universal House
251 Tottenham Court Road
London W1T 7AB
Tel + 44 (0)20 7813 3000
Fax + 44 (0)20 7813 6001
Email guides@timeout.com
www.timeout.com

EDITORIAL
Editor Hugh Graham
Listings Editor Cathy Limb
Proofreader Gill Harvey
Indexer Jackie Brind

Managing Director Peter Fiennes
Financial Director Gareth Garner
Editorial Director Sarah Guy
Series Editor Cath Phillips
Editorial Manager Holly Pick
Assistant Management Accountant
Ija Krasnikova

DESIGN
Art Director Scott Moore
Art Editor Pinelope Kourmouzoglou
Senior Designer Henry Elphick
Graphic Designer Gemma Doyle
Junior Graphic Designer Kei Ishimaru
Digital Imaging Simon Foster

PICTURE DESK
Picture Editor Jael Marschner
Deputy Picture Editor Katie Morris
Picture Researcher Helen McFarland

ADVERTISING
Sales Director/Sponsorship Mark Phillips
Sales Manager Alison Wallen

MARKETING
Group Marketing Director John Luck
Marketing Manager Yvonne Poon
Sales & Marketing Director, North America
Lisa Levinson

PRODUCTION
Group Production Director Mark Lamond
Production Manager Brendan McKeown
Production Controller Caroline Bradford

TIME OUT GROUP
Chairman Tony Elliott
Financial Director Richard Waterlow
Group General Manager/Director
Nichola Coulthard
Time Out Magazine Ltd MD Richard Waterlow
Managing Director, Time Out International
Cathy Runciman
TO Communications Ltd MD David Pepper
Group Art Director John Oakey
Group IT Director Simon Chappell

The editor would like to thank Cynthia Brouse, Robert Cocovinis, Michael Graham, Nancy Graham, Sarah Guy, Susan Guy, Kei Ishimaru, Tracey Kerrigan, Caroline Law, Jemima Lewis, John Macfarlane, Jane Marshall, Scott Moore, Jeremy O'Grady, Cath Phillips, Holly Pick, Caroline Robb, Eileen Whitfield, Elizabeth Winding and all the contributors to this book.

Maps Kei Ishimaru.

Photography
Front cover Beach huts in Whitby, North Yorkshire, UK ©Digital Vision Ltd/SuperStock.
Back cover Luksentyre, Alistair Keddie; Hell's Mouth, John Wormald.
Introduction page 1 Luksentyre, Alistair Keddie; page 3 Sandwood Bay, James Gordon; Sinclair Bay, James Gordon; page 6 Sandwood Bay, James Gordon; pages 6-7 West Wittering, Britta Jaschinski; page 7 Kynance Cove, Britta Jaschinski; Luksentyre, Alistair Keddie.

Pages 8-38, 97-125, 250, 251, 254 Britta Jaschinski; pages 49, 50, 52, 53, 56, 58-62, 65-68, 71 Walter Weber; pages 72, 74-76, 78, 79, 81-85, 87, 88, 90, 92, 95 Adam Burton; pages 129-136, 138, 139, 141, 142, 145, 146-151 Sam Robbins; pages 152, 154-157, 159 Mike Pinches; pages 160-165, 241-245, 247 Don Brownlow; pages 168, 170-172, 177-184, 186-188, 190 Andrew Kneath; page 175 Pembrokeshire County Council, Tourism & Leisure Services; pages 193-199 John Wormald; pages 200, 202, 204-207, 253, 255 Dennis Hardley; pages 209-215 Alistair Keddie; pages 216, 218-221, 225-229, 231, 252 James Gordon; pages 232, 234-239 Andy Hall.

Contents

Introduction

The tide is turning for the British seaside. Visitor numbers are up – by two million in the last three years – as are property prices. The travel sections are awash with headlines like 'Once more unto the beach' and 'We do like to be beside the seaside.' And *Coast*, the BBC television series, seems to be on permanent rotation; a glossy magazine of the same name was also launched in recent years.

It's a remarkable comeback. The British seaside had been dying a slow death for decades, ever since the rise of the foreign holiday; budget flights were supposed to be the final nail in the coffin. Who could resist fun in the sun – tropical seas, cocktails, whitewashed villas – when the alternative was windbreaks, tea from a thermos and *Fawlty Towers*. While holidaymakers were living it up on the Costa del Sol, British piers were crumbling and hotels were being boarded up. In the popular imagination, the British coast became more synonymous with gloomy Morrissey lyrics – 'this is the seaside town, they forgot to shut down' – than saucy postcards.

So what's changed? Perhaps global warming is playing a part: not only are people minding their carbon footprint and staying closer to home, the warmer temperatures – summer 2007 notwithstanding – make British beaches more enticing (and even when the weather reverts to miserable type, it's nice to be able to walk on a beach without fear of getting sunstroke). Britain has been cleaning up its act too. In the 1980s, only 20 British beaches were clean enough to merit a Blue Flag award; in 2007, 77 strands got the seal of approval. And gentrification is creeping to the coast, from Brighton's hip B&Bs to Cornwall's Jamie Oliver restaurant. Even tawdry Blackpool has opened its first boutique hotel. The British seaside, it seems, is slowly shedding its dowdy skin.

Not everyone craves a glossy sheen. A nostalgia kick is also fuelling the renaissance. The generation that grew up shivering beside their buckets and spades and eating fish

and chips by the pier wants to introduce their children to the same salty, time-honoured traditions. Travel trends are another factor: now that the masses are flying to Thailand, it almost seems passé. But making an epic journey to a wild and wonderful Scottish beach – now that's exotic.

Yet there's a simpler explanation for the revival: Britain's beaches are just plain gorgeous. Having seen the world on gap years and adventure holidays, people are starting to realise that some of the best beaches in the world are right here at home. They just couldn't see it for all the tired clichés and faraway visions of sun, sex and Sangría.

Speaking of clichés, this book steers clear of the usual end-of-the-pier suspects in favour of quiet charmers and undiscovered gems. It takes you to places that you never knew existed or can't get to on easyJet. The desert island dreams of the Hebrides, the Welsh postcards that put Cornwall in the shade, the Cornish coves that could pass for the Caribbean, the unsung castle coast of Northumberland, the sweeping East Anglian spectaculars, natural wonders along the south coast, northern comforts that are anything but grim and Robinson Crusoe idylls that are only a few hours from London. The best all-rounders and family favourites are thrown in for good measure. There are 30 intimate portraits in total, laid out in glorious technicolour, and more than 100 beaches described.

Not every beach included is a Blue Flag. But sometimes scenery trumps swimming, as in the case of Cornwall's Bedruthan Steps. Sometimes splendid isolation, as with Scotland's Sandwood Bay, holds more appeal than sunbathing. And sometimes, as with Dorset's Studland, you can have it all on one beach. Each one is living proof that the British coast can be lovelier – come rain or shine – than the tropical fantasies people spend their lives chasing. For once, the headlines are not all hype: we really do like to be beside the seaside. And paradise might be closer than you think.

Sennen Cove

Catch a wave at the end of the world.

'Of all the places I've been around the world, I still love coming home. This place is beautiful.' So says Sam Bleakley – one of Britain's few full-time professional surfers – of the village where he was brought up: Sennen Cove. During his career, Bleakley may have racked up a surf-travel CV that covers more than 35 countries – most of them little slices of paradise. But the magic of Sennen Cove, in the far west of Cornwall, unfailingly draws him back.

It is easy to see why. Tucked into the corner of Whitesand Bay on the Penwith peninsula, Sennen Cove is on the edge of Britain, a stone's throw from Land's End, with nothing but ocean between it and North America. And this feeling of isolation is what makes the place so special. Here, on mainland Britain's most westerly beach, the hordes have been left behind. Weathered houses are hatched into the hillside above the bay. A sweeping stretch of golden sands beckon. And the turquoise waters are dotted with dolphins, seals and basking sharks – not to mention surfers of a rather more chilled mien than in other parts of the UK.

The director Sam Peckinpah may have chosen the West Penwith peninsula as the setting for his iconic, ultra-violent *Straw Dogs* – the controversial 1971 thriller in which a young American man and his English wife are persecuted by a baying West Country mob. But the people of Sennen Cove are cut from a rather different cloth than the film's creepy characters. This is a coastal community, one where everyone's life is bound up in the sea

in some way. It is also a stronghold of 'free surfing' – the belief that grace, style and fun define a surfer, rather than aggression and competitive success.

Britain's surfing cognoscenti have long flocked to West Penwith. There is a saying among locals: 'If there's no swell here, there's none anywhere.' And they have a point. Facing north-west, the beach stretches in an arc from the southern end – by the village and esplanade – to Gwenver, a quiet area at the north end. To follow this trajectory is to go from beginners' waves to serious surf. Even in summer, there is usually a wave to be had; the beach takes the brunt of any swells driven by bands of low pressure in the Atlantic.

No wonder that the region was home to Britain's one and only surf camp. Funnily enough, in 1971, while Peckinpah was busy painting Penwith with his sinister brush, an ex-architect and trawlerman by the name of Chris Tyler was setting up the Skewjack Surf Village. Its counterculture animus, rather than the Peckinpah leitmotif of insularity and resentment, is what has persisted in these parts.

Skewjack, located a mile and a half from Sennen Cove in an old RAF shelter, enjoyed its heyday in the 1970s and early 1980s. Its tagline – 'Two girls for every boy!' – may not chime with today's politically correct zeitgeist, but Penwith locals still wax lyrical about wild parties at Skewjack and ensuing hungover surf trips to Sennen Cove. *The Times* visited Skewjack in 1971 and noted how its surfers were intent on 'a back-to-nature harmony with the sea'. It is this spirit – one of innocence – that has continued to infuse surfing in Sennen Cove, surviving Skewjack's closure in 1986.

Britain's surfing elite flocks to Sennen Cove, but there are waves for beginners too.

Even the local surf shop owner, Pat Dowling, sets his sights above the bottom line. He runs the Chapel Idne shop, fashioned entirely of natural timbers, on the site of a former chapel at the western end of the cove, and is known for his laid-back approach.

But there is more to Sennen Cove than surfing. Fishermen set forth from the Cove's small harbour every day – the village was once a major station for pilchard processing – and there is a proud gig-rowing tradition. The Cape Cornwall Pilot Gig Club enters teams each May in the World Gig Rowing Championships in the Scilly Isles.

There is also a lifeboat station dating back to 1853. And anyone who has ever visited Sennen Cove in a winter storm, when the spray from huge seas crashes over the cliffs of Pedn-men-du, will testify to the treachery of these waters.

But summer is a different story. To walk the coast path on a sun-kissed day from Gwenver, through the Cove and on to Land's End – just over a mile away – is to experience one of the most exquisite seascapes in the British Isles. On a clear day, the Scilly Isles can be seen. Mediterranean gulls, shearwaters, puffins, kingfishers and Arctic skua are the local aviators. Looking out to sea, you might see surfers paddling out to get up close and personal with dolphins and basking sharks; the latter are lured in by swarms of plankton rather than oceanic humans.

Amid so much peace, it is hard to believe that *Straw Dogs* was filmed nearby. Perhaps it's no coincidence that Peckinpah didn't venture to Sennen Cove. The surfers would have skewed his paranoid visions – and he might have made the feel-good movie of the year.

OTHER BEACHES

Porthcurno, three miles from Sennen Cove, regularly appears in 'Top Ten beach' lists. From the stone balustrades of the Minack Theatre (01736 810181, www.minack.com), carved into the cliffs above, you gaze upon a scene that is more Caribbean than Cornwall: wide white sands and brilliant seas in a sheltered cove. After a swim, watch a play in the open-air theatre, a local summer ritual. Across the bay there are ancient granite rocks, weathered by centuries of storms; at low tide an expanse of sand enables access to the nudist beach of Pedn Vounder. The sea seems even clearer here than at Sennen Cove. No wonder it is a summer haven for basking sharks – and also for local photographer Charles Roff, whose celebrated nudes were shot at Pedn. Less tantalising, but more importantly, Porthcurno was at one time the centre of the largest submarine cable telegraph station in the world. Owned by Cable & Wireless, the telegraph station operated as many as 14 cables and was of vital strategic importance to the Allies during World War II (Porthcurno Telegraph Museum, 01736 810966, www.porthcurno.org.uk).

If you crave seclusion, take a hike to Nanjizal beach, a 45-minute walk from the car park at Land's End. You'll probably have the place to yourself, unless you bump into a dog-walker – this is practically the only beach in the area where canine companions are allowed. But there are no lifeguards, so don't swim in rough seas. Nearer to Porthcurno, the tiny fishing village of Porthgwarra offers great atmosphere – and snorkelling – in its craggy cove. In fact, the whole coast, from Sennen Cove to Porthcurno, is a veritable Sea World, offering glimpses of seals, dolphins and, in summer, basking sharks.

WHERE TO STAY AND EAT

Built in the 17th century, the Old Success (01736 871232, www.oldsuccess.com) is a characterful fisherman's inn. Most of the 12 rooms have splendid views of Whitesand Bay; some have four-poster beds. The pub is down to earth, like the locals, and its menu is dominated by fresh local fish; Sunday roasts are recommended too.

Elsewhere in the Cove, just up from the harbour, there is traditional B&B accommodation at Myrtle Cottage (01736 871698), with lofty views and a seagull soundtrack. Its rustic café is popular for all-day breakfasts and fine Cornish cream teas.

Pengelly House (01736 871866, www.pengellyhouse.com), again just behind the esplanade, is another comfortable B&B – and a short walk from the beach. For more accommodation options, see www.sennen-cove.com.

Sennen Cove boasts one of Cornwall's best-placed restaurants. The aptly named Beach (01738 871191, www.thebeachrestaurant.com) is right on the sands, with a terrace overlooking Cape Cornwall. Owned by Phil Shannon, the UK's longest-serving lifeboat man, it is family-run and friendly. Though the decor is slick and modern, the natural wood lends a sense of warmth. Cornish-reared steak is a speciality; the seafood dishes – pollack, sole, lobster – are fresh and locally caught.

The Blue Lagoon (01736 871817), on the esplanade, is a classic chippie.

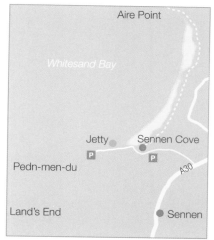

FACILITIES

Café. Ice-cream van (in summer). Toilets. Additional toilets/cafés at harbour end.

SPORTS

Surfing (lessons/board hire at Sennen Surfing Centre, Dave Muir, 01736 871 227, www.sennensurfingcentre.com; Smart Surf school, 01736 871817, www.smartsurf.co.uk).

SWIMMING

Safe in flat seas and small swells, particularly at the car park end, but the beach can be prone to rip tides. Seek advice from the lifeguards. Water quality: EC Guideline Standard/Good, according to Marine Conservation Society (MCS). But there is a filtered sewage discharge pipe in the area and potential for contamination, especially after storms.

HOW TO GET THERE

By car From Penzance, take the A30 to Land's End and turn off to Sennen Cove at Sennen. **By train** The nearest station is Penzance. **By bus** There is an hourly bus from Penzance and Porthcurno (01752 402060, www.firstgroup.com).

PARKING

Pay and display car parks at both ends of the esplanade. On the hill above the Cove, there is an additional pay and display car park, but it's a trek to the beach.

RULES

No dogs during summer.

FURTHER REFERENCE

Penzance Tourist Information Centre (01736 362207, www.penwith.gov.uk).

St Ives Bay

To the lighthouse.

Most people think they know St Ives. In the popular imagination, it's the quaint fishing village-cum-artist's colony, with a branch of the Tate, a Barbara Hepworth museum, whitewashed cottages and a couple of lovely sandy beaches, Porthmeor and Porthminster. But there's another St Ives. Less famous, but arguably more beautiful, St Ives Bay – to the north of the town – is a stunner: three miles of pristine sand, drawing a golden arc from the Godrevy Lighthouse in the north to the shimmering Hayle Estuary in the south. Its beauty has catapulted it into some illustrious company: it is a member of 'the Most Beautiful Bays in the World' club – an environmentally motivated, UNESCO-backed NGO – alongside the likes of San Francisco Bay, Cape Town's Table Bay and Venice Laguna.

It's not hard to see why. Backed by majestic cliffs, lapped by Caribbean-blue waters and bathed in the same ethereal light as its artsy neighbour, this pearly crescent is wildly romantic. You've probably seen artist renderings on greeting cards or posters, and thought it was in the tropics. You may have read about it, too: Godrevy Beach is thought to be the inspiration for Virginia Woolf's *To the Lighthouse*.

Facing St Ives town across the water, the lighthouse – erected in 1859 – stands on Godrevy Island, a rocky islet where seabirds natter and seals come to fish. Back on the mainland, the birds' incessant clamour rises from the cliff faces at Godrevy Point, an avian stopover – for fulmars, oystercatchers, cormorants, guillemots, gannets and razor-bills – and photographer's perch (it is a prime spot for watching sunsets).

Down on the beach, wildlife mingles with humans. Beachcombers hunt the rock pools for crabs, dogwhelks, anemones and starfish; climbers and birds share rocky outcrops; surfers watch out for basking sharks, dolphins and seals.

Gwithian, south of Godrevy, is another surfers' paradise. Like its northerly neighbour, it catches the swells that blow in from the open Atlantic, and has similar terrain: coarse sands, rugged cliff faces and great slate stacks. Gwithian village, too, is quintessentially Cornish. Half a mile inland, it is filled with farm shops, gardens serving cream teas, thatched cottages and a village pub.

Back on the beach, the rugged landscape softens with every step south. A maze of 'towans' – Cornish for sand hills – backs the shore, starting at Gwithian. These silky mounds are knitted together by marram grass and a tangle of footpaths, some part of the South West Coast Path; when the tide comes in, parts of the beach disappear, but walkers can traverse the entire length of the strand in the dunes. Naturalists may prefer to do so: a designated Site of Special Scientific Interest, the towans host myriad flora and fauna, from wild iris and pyramidal orchids, to butterflies, adders and skylarks. Romantics, meanwhile, sculpt armchairs on the sandy peaks to watch the sunset.

The surf peters out as you walk south. In the bay's sheltered south-western elbow, at Hayle Towans, fishing boats putter along the glassy estuary. While the surfers are in full swing up in Godrevy and Gwithian, Hayle Towans is a mecca for kitesurfers. But the action doesn't stop when the wind dies down: kayakers dot the shoreline here, while families play on the huge sheet of fine sand, swim in gentle seas warmed by the Gulf Stream or watch trains rumble along the coastal railway across the estuary.

Behind the harbour, the sprawling town of Hale is slowly shedding its slightly dated skin. A few trendy bars have sprung up, along with a smattering of boutiques, a funky ice-cream bar and an art gallery. The seafront pub at Hayle Towans, by contrast, still has an air of Butlins about it, drawing clientele from the beachside caravans.

But you don't come to St Ives Bay for wining and dining – the famous town across the water fills that niche. Nor do you come for culture, Virginia Woolf notwithstanding. While tourists are crowding the Tate and popping into galleries in the town, visitors to the Bay are stepping into a real life landscape painting. Welcome to the other St Ives.

OTHER BEACHES

When the tide is out, it is easy to mistake Porthkidney Sands – a sheltered gem of a beach – for an extension of St Ives Bay; its golden flats are separated from Hayle beach by a narrow tongue of water. But be warned: the river estuary is deep and dangerous to cross. It is made for boats and not for paddling, so you can only access the beach via the cliffs and dunes. Away from the river mouth, the rest of the beach is a beauty for swimming, with plenty of room for sunbathers and dog-walkers at low tide. Surfers flock here during the winter; when storms flatten other breakers in the area, the waves at Porthkidney are still clean and ridable, owing to the beach's sheltered position.

While the beach at St Ives Bay is vast, open and wild, the beaches of St Ives town are manicured plots of sand chiselled into the landscape. Still, the summer crowds can do nothing to puncture the pristine beauty of Porthmeor and Porthminster, both of which

There are three miles of sand at St Ives Bay: plenty of room to spread out or run wild.

have been awarded Blue Flag status. Pounded by Atlantic swell, Porthmeor is a popular surfing beach, backed by Tate St Ives (possibly the only museum to have a surfboard rack for visitors). The palm-fringed Porthminster, meanwhile, is a favourite of bathers and foodies – the Porthminster Café (01736 7953520) has got tongues wagging.

WHERE TO STAY AND EAT

For a front-row sea view, the bohemian Beach House (01736 332487, www.chycor.co.uk/cottages) is a cool, self-catering home with sandy Hayle on its doorstep. Next door, Penellen Guest House (01736 753777, www.golds-hire.co.uk) is not as hip, but the B&B boasts the same great vistas.

In the heart of the towans, the Sandbanks (01736 332487, www.chycor.co.uk) is the stuff of beach hut fantasies, with loads of character: blue-and-white timber exterior, quirky nautical features and driftwood details.

Live out your Virginia Woolf fantasies at Calize Country House, (01736 753268, www.calize.co.uk): it has sweeping views of Godrevy Lighthouse and bay. The 1870s manor house, above the village of Gwithian, boasts four decadent en suite rooms and sumptuous home-cooked breakfasts.

For cool camping, go under the canvas at Churchtown Farm Campsite, where spacious pitches are steps away from the surf and the milkman will deliver papers and provisions (01736 753219, www.churchtownfarm.org.uk). For more accommodation, see www.gwithian.org.uk/accomodation.htm.

The Godrevy Beach Café (01736 757999) puts your average beach kiosk to shame. You can chill out on the upper deck and stare at the ocean. And junk food is replaced by organic coffees, delectable cakes, wholesome lunches or candlelit dinners.

The funky new Sandsifter (01736 758457, www.sandsiftergodrevy.co.uk), also at Godrevy, is geared towards the cool, surfy crowd. The bar and restaurant are spruced up to the max, and there is a sun deck, fab cocktail list and surf shop to boot.

A stone's throw inland, but worlds away in feel, Gwithian's Red River Inn (01736 753223, www.red-river-inn.com) is a cosy village pub with a modern culinary twist. Expect local ales, good wines and delicious dishes made with ingredients plucked from the doorstep.

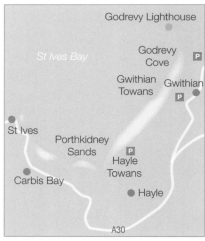

HOW TO GET THERE

By car When you are driving south in Cornwall, come off the A30 at the Loggans Moor (Hayle) exit. For Godrevy and Gwithian, turn right at the first mini roundabout and follow the B3301. For Hayle Towans, head over the mini roundabout, through the traffic lights, and turn right by the recreation grounds (signposted Phillack and the Beaches). **By train** The London-to-Penzance line stops at Hayle; the station is about a mile from Hayle Towans. **By bus** The Truro-St Ives service stops at Hayle (01752 402060, www.firstgroup.com); Western Greyhound services run from Penzance to Hayle, Gwithian and Godrevy (01637 871871, www.westerngrey hound.com).

PARKING

Pay parking Easter-Oct at Godrevy, Gwithian and Hayle Towans (NT members free at Godrevy). Free Nov-Easter.

FACILITIES

Cafés. Lost children points. Toilets (disabled, baby-changing facilities) at Godrevy, Gwithian and Hayle Towans. National Trust hut at Godrevy (area warden 01872 552412, www.nationaltrust.org.uk).

SPORTS

Kitesurfing (Mobius Kite School, 08456 430630, www.mobiusonline.co.uk). Surfing (Gwithian Surf Academy, 01736 755493, www.surfacademy. co.uk; Shore Surf School, 01736 755556, www.shoresurf.com).

SWIMMING

Stay between red and yellow flags. Beware of undertows at Hayle Estuary, Red River (Godrevy). Lifeguards at Godrevy and Hayle May-Sept. Water quality: MCS recommended. But there is potential for sewage contamination at Godrevy/Hayle in extreme weather.

RULES

No campfires, camping, jet skis. No dune boards, mountain boards and motorbikes in the dunes. No dogs Easter-1 Oct at main areas – Hayle Towans, Gwithian and Godrevy. Dogs permitted in designated areas – Mexico Towans, Phillack Towans and Upton Towans.

FURTHER REFERENCE

Websites: www.go-cornwall.com; www.nationaltrust.org.uk; www. penwith.gov.uk; www.stives-cornwall.co.uk.

Bedruthan Steps

The jagged edge.

Cornwall is famous for its rocky coast, but Bedruthan Steps takes the cragginess to extremes. Here, the beach plays second fiddle to the towering rock stacks, each one a talking point. Some are chiselled and pointy like pyramids, others resemble barnacle-encrusted turrets. Legend says they were once the stepping stones of a giant, and it's easy to feel small and insignificant in such a dramatic landscape – one of the wildest beaches of the West Country, just up the coast from Newquay.

Standing on top of the rugged cliffs, you can literally watch the scenery being carved. With the ocean pummelling the cliffs, new rocky outcrops are gradually being formed by the constant crumbling. In such turbulent surroundings, the terrain is always changing. In 1980, for instance, the distinctive crown of the Queen Bess rock stack was lost to the raging seas. And visitors are advised to steer clear of the cliff edges – both above and below – which are gradually collapsing. Closed from November to February, Cornwall's stormiest season, Bedruthan Steps is not for the faint-hearted – even in clement weather. The steep path down to the beach might induce vertigo and the return journey will give your lungs a workout. Though currently well maintained, the steps have fallen away in the past and have also closed several times owing to structural work and cliff stabilisation. Not exactly a gentle stroll down the promenade, then. But oh, the scenery.

At low tide, the sand is a glittering backdrop to Cornwall's jagged rock stars. Starting at Carnewas Point, the beach wends its way seductively around the craggy statues for about a mile. Park Head, the peninsula on the horizon, lends some solidity to the crumbling landscape. The stony sculptures are besieged by armies of mussels and topped by mossy hats and seagulls. The rockpools and caves, meanwhile, are quintessential Cornwall; the echo of the sea resounds in the cliff's caverns. But as you get swept away by the romance of it all, don't get swept away by the incoming tide.

At high tide, waves spray the boulders and much of the beach disappears. Don't even think about swimming or surfing here. Though a few hardened locals do bring their boards, they take their life in their hands: Bedruthan Steps is very much a case of beauty with cruelty. The currents are treacherous and the rocks can be deadly. Before Trevose lighthouse was erected in 1847, this stretch of coast was notorious for shipwrecks. Samaritan Island, one of the rocks on the beach, got its name from a wreck in 1846, when the brig *Samaritan* ran aground. Despite the tragedy, the crag was dubbed 'The Good Samaritan' by locals – and no wonder: they dressed themselves in robes and fineries salvaged from the ship's cargo.

Water sports are out, then, but walking is in. You can bring your dog here. And if the stone staircase is too perilous, take in the scene from the South West Coast Path above. It's a sure way to avoid the dangers of the incoming sea and arguably a better photo opportunity. Gentle on the legs yet powerful in its drama, the cliff-top walk between Carnewas Point and Park Head serves up beauty on a plate. In spring and summer, a riot of wildflowers dots the hedgerows. Cornfields sweep inland next to sheer cliffs with 300-foot drops. Grassy burrows on the headland are tailor-made for picnics. If you can bear

The stormy seas are not for swimming, but the cliff paths are made for walking.

to concentrate on anything, look out for cormorants, petrels, shags and guillemots in the rocky crags. If you're lucky, you might spot the odd puffin. Completing the Cornish picture, the remains of Redcliff Castle – an Iron Age fort – are scattered near the path.

In splendid isolation, Bedruthan Steps has one hidden neighbour: Mawgan Porth, a beach resort tucked into the next valley. It's a good place to take a dip or stock up on supplies. Bedruthan Steps only has the occasional ice-cream van, and a tea shop in the old counting house of the Carnewas tin mine.

Despite the aforementioned legend of the giant, the mine may actually have given Bedruthan Steps its name. One theory posits that the moniker is derived from the ladder, or steps, down the mine. Yet, in a landscape where you are dwarfed by nature, it is easier to believe the story of the behemoth – only a giant could make you feel this small.

OTHER BEACHES

The waves may lash the gnarled rocks at Bedruthan Steps, but at Mawgan Porth they kiss the golden sands – and invite the surfers out to play. The breakers here are less crowded than at neighbouring Newquay, making them ideal for beginners. And what with soft white sands, rock pools, surf schools and dramatic sunsets – which can be viewed from seaside watering holes – this is a good one for a proper day at the beach, and more accessible than neighbouring Bedruthan.

Not only is Watergate Bay one of Cornwall's most beautiful beaches, it is a mecca for water sports. Here, you can ride the waves and master the arts of kitesurfing and wave-skiing, or simply watch the beach action from Jamie Oliver's Fifteen Cornwall (see p31) or the chilled-out Beach Hut bistro (01637 860840). The bay is just south of Bedruthan Steps.

North of the Steps, Porthcotan offers a dramatic sequel to its neighbour. Marking the most southerly of 'the seven bays' – a string of sandy coves that lace the cliffs

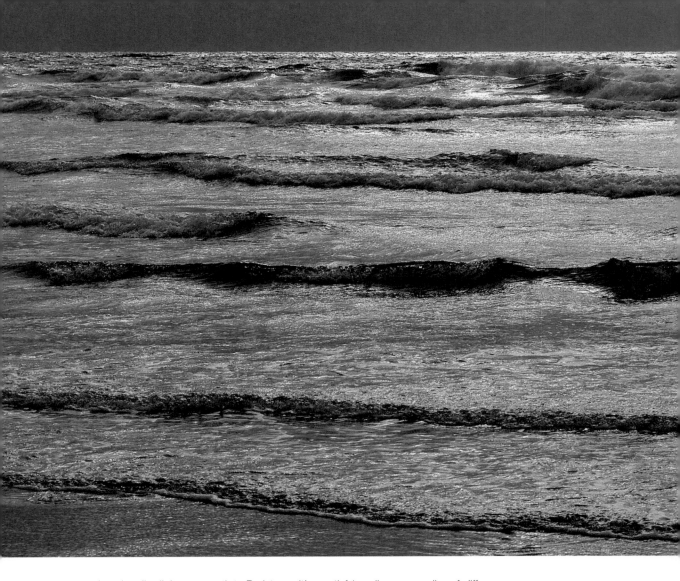

together virtually all the way north to Padstow – it's a satisfying climax: a medley of cliffs, caves and blowholes. Other highlights along the string of bays include the skeletal remnants of a German war ship at Booby's Bay, the pristine white sands of Mother Ivey's Bay (named after a farmer's widow who claimed the rights to all the shipwreck booty along this part of the coast) and the breakers bulldozing into Constantine and Treyarnon – two more surfers' favourites.

WHERE TO STAY AND EAT

If you want a sea view, you might just have to sleep outside. During July and August, you can pitch a tent in a cliff-top location at Bedruthan Steps Camping (01637 860943) – a big field with basic (yet spotless) facilities.

The only year-round option within spitting distance of the sand is the chintzy Bedruthan House Hotel (01637 860346, www.bedruthanhousehotel.co.uk). The Bedruthan

Steps Hotel (01637 860555, www.bedruthan.com), by contrast, is more sophisticated, and only a three-minute drive or bus ride to the beach. With its eco-credentials, stylishly simple rooms, sea views, chic bar and restaurant, and a pool and a spa too, it's an all-round winner – if a little too family-friendly for some.

For something more intimate, bag one of the three garden suites or a cool surf-style lodge at the Blue Bay Lodge Hotel (01637 860324, www.bluebaycornwall.co.uk).

Perched on the cliff-tops in the National Trust car park, the Carnewas Tearoom combines views with cosy nostalgia, serving cream teas, cakes and sandwiches in a stone hut (01637 860701). For fresh Cornish produce, innovative menus and a chic beachside venue, you don't have to go far: Jamie Oliver's Fifteen Cornwall (01637 861000, www. fifteencornwall.co.uk) is just ten minutes away at Watergate Bay, and the rather swanky Fire (01637 860372) has recently opened at Mawgan Porth. True to its name, flambé cooked at your table is Fire's signature special, and the exotic twist on local ingredients will give Oliver's chefs a run for their money.

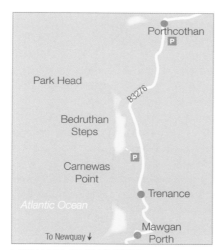

HOW TO GET THERE

By car Bedruthan Steps is just off the B2376 (Newquay to Padstow coast road). **By train** Newquay station is seven miles away. **By bus** Western Greyhound runs a Newquay to Padstow bus service (556) via the airport (01637 871871, www.westerngreyhound. com). **By air** Newquay airport is about ten minutes by taxi/car/bus (01637 860600, www.newquaycornwall airport.com).

PARKING

Two pay car parks; both about a five-minute walk to the viewpoint and staircase. Both £2 (NT members free with card at Carnewas, the parking lot to the south).

FACILITIES

Café. Shop (01637 860563). Toilet (including disabled).

SWIMMING

No swimming or water sports owing to dangerous currents and rocks. No lifeguards or emergency facilities. Area warden (01841 540540). Water quality: not MCS tested.

RULES

No barbecues, fires. Dogs permitted all year round. Cliff staircase closed 1 Nov-28 Feb.

FURTHER REFERENCE

Websites: www.cornwalltouristboard. co.uk; www.restormel.gov.uk. Local council (www.ncdc.gov.uk).

Praa Sands

The family jewel.

Praa Sands may be one of West Cornwall's most popular beaches, but it suffers from something of an identity crisis. In terms of geography, some people consider it part of the Lizard, others part of the Penwith peninsula. In terms of star quality, it lacks the romance of some of its Cornish brethren (a Kynance Cove, say, or a St Ives). And as for consumption, Praa is not exactly a glamourpuss: it lacks a hotel and a promenade, and its small array of beachfront shops is sufficiently weathered as to almost cry out for a lick of paint (if not a wholesale redesign).

But that is the point of Praa Sands. This is an unpretentious, honest and lovely English beach, one where having a bucket and spade is far more important than sporting a fake tan and wearing the latest surfing gear (though it is, in the right conditions, beloved of wave riders). It's not exactly a slouch in the looks department, either: a mile-long stretch of gold sand, backed by dunes, with rocky outcrops at either end. Favoured by families, it boasts clean water and good swimming; the unaffected, easy-going vibe is another draw. What's more, its ambiguous, neither-here-nor-there location just adds to the appeal: it's a good jumping off point for trips into the rest of Cornwall, with Land's End and Penzance to the west, St Ives to the north, and Lizard Point to the east. In other words, a fine base for a family holiday.

Yet Praa Sands (pronounced 'pray') has another quirky – and very English – string to its bow: this is a great place for beach cricket. At low tide, in particular, its flat sands are tailor-made for a sandy match. And if you notice one of the bowlers on the beach blowing his batsmen out of the water, chances are it is Chris Old, the former England cricketer, who has made his home here and become a local fixture. Old relocated to Praa Sands in 1992, and opened a restaurant and chippie overlooking the beach. Cricket fans might find themselves sitting at a table in the garden of his Clipper restaurant, contemplating the expanse of sand at low tide, and remembering England's past sporting glories.

Cricket aside, it is surfing that really put Praa Sands on the map. The summer boarding hordes may flock to Cornwall's north coast, but, on the right swell and especially in winter, Praa Sands is the place to be. Facing south-west, the beach picks up more swell than its more sheltered neighbours within Mount's Bay. In fact, the combination of south-westerly and north-westerly swells can create some of the best waves in Cornwall; clean barrels can be ridden on just about all states of the tide. There is just one downside: everyone knows about the surf at Praa, so when it's good, there is fierce competition for waves.

Some of the surfers may be practising for one of Praa Sands' more obscure claims to fame. The beach hosts the intriguingly named World Crap Surfing Championships, an event that does what it says on the tin. Held sporadically, usually in the month of December, the event discourages surfers of even modest ability. If you can barely stand up on a board, then, Praa Sands could allow you to add 'Have competed in a World Championship' to your CV.

Surfers – whether wholly unskilled, expert or somewhere in between – are catered for by Stones Reef Surf Shop, right on the beach. It nestles underneath one of the county's best post-surf hangouts, the Sandbar, a place whose airy and modern Mediterranean ambience makes its former incarnation – a down-at-heel 1970s disco – hard to imagine. Even before its makeover, though, the Sandbar was a wonderful place to gaze at the Atlantic – an ocean of serenity in the summer and a cauldron of wild storms in winter. At high tide, the sea is so close, the waves almost lap at the Sandbar's patio.

The beach's surfing credentials, however, are rivalled by its natural ones. Even a layperson will be able to appreciate its geological significance. A third of the way along the beach, there is a black platform at the base of the dunes, which geologists (and there are often a few wandering around) will tell you is actually a 1,300-year-old-peat bed made up of decayed forest (the beach was designated a Regionally Important Geological/Geomorphical site in 1995). Then there's the requisite bird life – migrants stopping off on their way to and from Africa include terns, auks and gannets – and wildlife in the form of rabbits and badgers, which scurry around blackthorn, bramble and elder scrub (not to mention dolphins and porpoises in the sea).

There's a touch of culture too. Pengersick castle dates back to 1500, and is reputedly one of the most haunted places in Britain.

But you don't need to be a geologist, a surfer, a cricketer, or still less a ghostbuster, to appreciate Praa Sands. If you're a parent, all you need is a bucket and spade for sandcastles, and a net to catch crabs in the rock pools. If you've outgrown such practices, Praa offers a no-frills break that's low on glitz and glamour, and high on natural, unspoiled beauty – and understated English charm.

With its good swimming and easy-going vibe, Praa is a favourite with families.

OTHER BEACHES

If the surf's up, Perranuthnoe (just a few miles along the coast towards Penzance) offers marginally less crowded conditions. Like Praa, Perranuthnoe has beachbreak surf, working on big south-westerly swells held up by a north-easterly wind. It also boasts a reef break, known as the 'cabbage patch,' at the eastern end of the bay. High tide is not the time to come for a surf – the beach has all but disappeared.

A walk to Prussia Cove – actually a group of isolated coves along the coast path – is a must. The romance of the landscape is enhanced by its history. The cove was named after John Carter, alias the King of Prussia, a notorious smuggler. Carter got his nickname as a boy, when he played soldiers on the beach and pretended to be the Prussian monarch. As an adult, his rich pickings were stashed away in Piskies and Bessy's Coves; between them lie an iron post and chains, relics of the HMS *Warspite*, the largest wreck ever to occur on the Cornish coast, back in 1947. Further afield, there is another excellent walk from Marazion, across the sand at low tide, to the medieval castle of St Michael's Mount.

WHERE TO STAY AND EAT

In keeping with its understated appeal, Praa Sands does not have a single hotel. There are, however, a few B&Bs. One of the best is Dingley Dell (01736 763527, www.dingley dell.eu), a white bungalow on the way into Praa. It's set in mature gardens and also offers a light-filled self-catering studio. There's also caravan accommodation at the Praa Sands Holiday Park. But the most beautiful place to stay is nearby Prussia Cove (01736 762014, www.prussiacove.co.uk), offering get-away-from-it-all digs amid sandy coves and wild scenery. There, the Porth-en-Alls private family estate comprises numerous cottages and houses for rent. There are no ice-cream kiosks – and no roads (access is via footpaths with cars left in a small car park). For more information on where to stay, visit www.chycor.co.uk and www.cornwall-online.co.uk.

The beach is better served for food. Chris Old's Clipper Restaurant (01736 763751, www.chrisold.co.uk) serves traditional English fare with an emphasis on fresh fish, complemented by sea views and outdoor seating. There is another café right on the beach (the Beachcomber), but a better bet is the Sandbar (01736 793516, www.sandbarpraasands.co.uk). Its 1970s disco past has thankfully been eclipsed by slick decor, fresh seafood, locally sourced fillet steaks and a hearty Sunday lunchtime carvery.

HOW TO GET THERE

By car Approaching from the north-east on the A30 at Hayle, follow the directions to Penzance. Shortly after Crowlas take the first left on a roundabout onto the A394. After about six miles, turn right to Praa Sands. Alternatively, approach from Helston on the A394. **By train** The nearest train station is Penzance. **By bus** There are buses to the beach from Helston or Penzance (0871 200 2233, www.truronian.co.uk).

PARKING

Two pay car parks at west end of beach. Beware of clampers in the area.

FACILITIES

Campsite. Café/restaurant. Caravan park. First-aid post. Lost child centre. Pub. Shops. Slipway. Toilets (disabled). Note: the amenities are at the western end of the beach.

SPORTS

Diving. Surfing. Waterskiing. Windsurfing (for all water sports, contact Stones Reef Diving & Water Sports, 01736 76299).

SWIMMING

Good swimming. Lifeguards (01736 762734) present at the western end from third week of May-mid Sept. Rest of the year: lifeguard service weekends and school holidays. Emergency facilities. Water quality: MCS recommended.

RULES

No camping. No dogs Easter-Oct. Horses permitted. Check signs regarding bonfires and barbecues.

FURTHER REFERENCE

Penzance Tourist Information (01736 362207 or 01872 322900, www.cornwalltouristboard.co.uk). Local council (www.kerrier.gov.uk).

Kynance Cove

Into the blue.

It's easy to miss Kynance Cove. Many visitors to Cornwall, if they get as far as the Lizard Peninsula, gravitate inexorably to Lizard Point, Britain's southernmost spot. In their quest, they ignore the discreet turning on the right: the road to Kynance Cove. After being photographed at the Lizard Lighthouse, the masses head back to Penzance – and the tried-and-true tourist trail.

This is a mistake. Kynance Cove may not be the place to hire pedaloes, surfboards and deckchairs. And getting there might involve something of a walk. But it is, without doubt, the jewel in the Lizard's crown.

Remote, wild and craggy, characterised by sea-blue serpentine and an ever-present sense of solitude, the cove is a place of extraordinary beauty – and a piece of vintage Cornish landscape. In fact, 'Kynans' means gorge in the Cornish language. And this particular gorge is backed by 200-foot cliffs and scattered with characterful stacks, pinnacles, arches, caves and rock pools, all set against turquoise waters. In the right light, the combination of brilliant seas, pinkish sands and dramatic rocks calls to mind Bermuda, *The Tempest* and any number of treasure islands.

It is no surprise, then, that this painterly setting has lured artists down the ages, including, most famously, William Holman Hunt. One of the original Pre-Raphaelites, and obsessed with colour, Hunt was naturally taken with the cove.

In 1860, Hunt visited the cove with Alfred, Lord Tennyson, on a walking holiday. The latter wrote of its 'glorious grass' and 'green monsters of waves'. Hunt, meanwhile, produced a pencil and watercolour called *Asparagus Island*. The work is characterised by a joie de vivre that was more typical of the later French Fauvist movement than Pre-Raphaelite rigour. It displays a sense of lightness and delicacy, and was hailed by critics for depicting sunlight in a sophisticated way. Kynance Cove hasn't changed much since 1860; in such an exquisite place, it's easy to see how Hunt escaped the hard, heavy complexity that was de rigueur in his day.

In fact, Asparagus Island is no mere fancy but a real place, within a stone's throw of the cove. Wild asparagus, a spiky flowering plant that only grows in a handful of places, flourishes on this hump of rock. It can be reached on foot via the Bellows, a stretch of white sand evident at low tide.

Remote, wild and craggy, Kynance Cove is a haven for rare birds and romantic souls.

Similarly rare is the chough, a bird with distinctive scarlet legs and bill. It disappeared from the Lizard in 1952, but returned here to breed in 2002. Cornwall's county emblem features the chough, and along the coast, at Lizard Point, there is a dedicated viewing point for devotees of the jet-black bird.

Walking – whether to see the chough or merely to gaze abstractly at the sea beneath the coast path – is a major reason to visit Kynance Cove. The jagged coastline blossoms with wild flowers in the summer and oozes drama when the sea crashes in during winter storms. To walk from the idyllic Mullion Cove, through Kynance Cove and on to Lizard Point, is to encounter an elemental landscape. Here, the serpentine rock is majestic, the seas are rarely still and the soul is easily stirred.

But Kynance can also make for a lovely day at the beach. At low tide, there are sandy nooks and crannies galore. Indeed, the combination of caves, rock pools and sugary sand is the stuff of childhood fantasy. And though the currents can be strong, people have been bathing in these azure seas since Victorian times (Prince Albert brought his children here on holiday in 1846). On a calm day, having a splash or a body surf in these sparkling

waters, surrounded by so much beauty, is a joy. If, however, there is mild to moderate swell, and the tide is high, swimmers – especially children – should take care: it is easy to be lulled into a false sense of security by all the prettiness.

The scenery makes up for the lack of entertainment. Don't come here expecting amusement arcades; do come if you want to know what Wordsworth meant when he wrote of poetry being 'emotion recollected in tranquility'. Because other than a café, and remnants of Bronze and Iron Age settlements, there is nothing here – nothing, that is, except dazzling seas, glittering sands, ancient, storm-lashed rocks and newly formed rock pools. And, above all, that wonderful sense of solitude.

It is no surprise that Holman Hunt, known for his didactic style, all but escaped the fetters of his characteristic hard-edged precision while painting here. If there is anywhere that will set your spirit free, it is this secretive cove. Lizard Point may be Britain's most southerly spot, but Kynance Cove is arguably its prettiest.

OTHER BEACHES

In bad weather, storm chasers should make a beeline for Porthleven (north of Kynance Cove). Watching the breakers crash over its high sea wall is a thrilling spectacle. If the wind happens to be blowing offshore, this is also a good place to watch surfers in action – Porthleven offers some of England's best waves. That's because the reef to the north-west of the harbour creates perfect tubing waves, which are surfed by a hardcore group of locals. Visiting surfers make a pilgrimage here too, but this is a dangerous place for novices.

Poldhu Cove, south from Porthleven, is a fine beach. It's a large, sandy cove, with a bit of dune action, and lifeguard cover during the summer. Its main claim to fame, however, is the Poldhu Wireless Station, from which Guglielmo Marconi sent the first transatlantic wireless signal in 1901. The remains can still be seen along the rugged cliffs above the beach.

Kennack Sands, on the east side of the Lizard, offers good bathing and is popular with families. It's got a generous stretch of golden sand, backed up by a fair share of crag and rock pools to keep the scenery interesting.

The nearby fishing village of Cagdwith is an old smugglers' cove with a wonderful 300-year-old pub (01326 290513, www.cadgwithcoveinn.com).

WHERE TO STAY AND EAT

There are no hotels at Kynance Cove, but there is one lone cottage near the café, overlooking the beach. It has one bedroom and a sofa bed; in the winter, a coal stove in the living room lends cosiness (01326 290436, www.kynancecovecottage.co.uk).

The Mullion Cove Hotel (01326 240328, www.mullioncove.com), a few miles north, makes for a wonderful base to explore Kynance Cove and the Lizard. Set on the cliffs above the working harbour of Mullion Cove, the hotel provides spectacular views. Built at the behest of the Cornish Railway at the turn of the century, it feels traditional and Edwardian; one suspects that Holman Hunt would have been at home here.

The Polurrian Hotel (01326 240421, www.polurrianhotel.com), also in Mullion, boasts 12 acres of landscaped gardens and its own private sandy beach, topped off by a sun terrace, three lounges and a games room. The hotel restaurant, the High Point, benefits from staggering views of the Atlantic (from which a good deal of its menu will have been freshly caught).

Kynance Cove has an eponymous café (www.kynancecovecafe.co.uk), offering largely traditional fare and seating both inside and out. In keeping with the natural vibe, it is solar powered and has a living turf roof.

For a memorable meal, drive north along the coast to the port of Porthleven. Kota Restaurant (01326 562407) serves English cuisine (much of it fresh seafood) with an Asian twist. The surroundings are relaxed and comfortable.

You can't come to Cornwall without eating a pasty. They are ten a penny around these parts, but the Lizard Pasty Shop (Beacon Terrace, 01326 290889), run by Ann Muller at Lizard Point, makes the best batches this side of Penzance.

At low tide, there are sandy nooks and crannies galore, with a cluster of caves and rock pools for exploring.

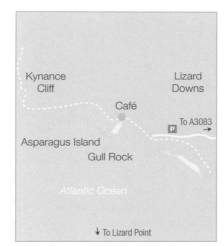

Kynance
Cliff

Lizard
Downs

Café

To A3083
P →

Asparagus Island
Gull Rock

Atlantic Ocean

↓ To Lizard Point

HOW TO GET THERE

By car From Helston, take the A3083 to Lizard town. Kynance Cove is signposted and on the right, about a mile before Lizard Point. **By bus** The Truronian T3 Helston–Kynance Cove runs from June-Oct only (with connections from Redruth); otherwise take the T1 Perranporth–Lizard. Make sure it's the bus that passes Truro, before reaching Kynance Cove (01872 273453, www.truronian.co.uk).

PARKING

National Trust pay car park at Kynance and Lizard Point. Ten-minute walk from Kynance car park. Steep steps at the end.

FACILITIES

Café. Shop. Toilets at car park (nappy-changing facilities).

SWIMMING

People swim or splash in calm seas, but there are rip tides and strong currents. No lifeguard. The tide sweeps in fast and can strand. Water quality: no sewage, but not MCS tested.

RULES

No barbecues, camping or fires. No dogs Easter-Sept.

FURTHER REFERENCE

Helston and Lizard Peninsula Tourist Information (01326 281481, www.cornwalltouristboard.co.uk). National Trust (01326 561407, www.nationaltrust.org.uk). Local council (www.kerrier.gov.uk).

Saunton Sands

The miracle miles.

Crowded beaches take all the fun out of the seaside. It's hard to relax surrounded by row after row of scorched pink bodies packed tight like sausages in a pan, a sight never seen in the wide-open, sandy spaces of North Devon. Here, gorse-covered headlands rush pell-mell to the sea's edge, their craggy forms framing mile upon mile of deserted sand. From Woolacombe to Westward Ho!, vast, spectacular beaches are the norm and Saunton Sands – with its pale gilt sands, big skies and invigoratingly salty sea breeze – is one of the finest. These are wild, romantic, shipwrecking shores. Atlantic swell pounds the beach with huge white rollers, providing a constant background roar and producing a fine white mist above the waves. These impressive breakers lure surfers and bodyboarding families in equal numbers. Yet no matter how many people come, the three-mile stretch never gets congested. Whether it's high summer or a windswept New Year's Day, Saunton offers solitude and serenity of the kind more often found in the Hebrides. To top it off, the beach is backed by enormous dunes: Braunton Burrows are the largest in Britain.

With a vista this good, it's not surprising that film-makers have discovered Saunton's panoramic possibilities. The beach was first used in 1946 for the Powell and Pressburger film, *A Matter of Life and Death*. It stars in the opening sequence, when David Niven's character survives his parachuteless jump and is washed up on the beach, which he mistakes for heaven. Later, it was used as a double for the Normandy landing scenes in the 1982 Pink Floyd film, *The Wall*. Pink Floyd returned to deposit 800 NHS beds on the beach for the cover picture of their 1987 album, *A Momentary Lapse of Reason*; more recently, Robbie Williams filmed his 'Angels' video here.

On this windswept beach, it's easy to feel as though you're in a movie yourself – an epic, no less. Leave behind the families, clustered around the row of brightly painted beach huts or behind the striped windbreaks, and seek solitude further down, where dogs run free and so do your spirits. The only sign of civilisation is the Saunton Sands Hotel, a big block of white against the dark, gorse-covered headland. Out to sea, unspoiled Lundy Island provides an effective barometer (a clear outline means rain tomorrow) and the opportunity of a day trip (from Ilfracombe) if the charms of beach life fade.

Braunton Burrows, however, are the biggest diversion. For children, the huge mounds are the perfect place to run, slide and scream. It's an exciting place for nature-lovers too. In 2004, a vast swathe of the dunes was designated a UNESCO Biosphere (an area of outstanding natural diversity), joining the likes of Mount Vesuvius and the Danube Delta. The frequently flooded interior nourishes more than 500 species of wild flower and plant, many rare. Children can look out for the viper's bugloss (*echium vulgare*), whose purple calyxes resemble a snake's head with its tongue sticking out; the foredunes are dotted with the pale mauve flowers of sea stock (*matthiola sinuata*); the nodding yellow heads of evening primrose grace the inner dunes. Orchids love the limey soil and damp hollows.

Botanists rub shoulders with twitchers, as migrating birds use the Burrows to rest and feed. There are large flocks of waders and waterfowl on the estuary as well as magpies, skylarks, meadow pipits, hovering kestrels and, inland, the odd buzzard.

The combination of stillness and fierce natural beauty doesn't just attract naturalists. In the aftermath of World War I, the region provided solace for one of North Devon's most famous literary sons, Henry Williamson, author of *Tarka the Otter*. He described the dunes as an 'Arabian desert in miniature… a place of the spirit of aloneness… sense of time and place is lost and a man becomes a spirit of sea and air and sky, feeling the everlastingness of life'. Williamson wrote *Tarka* in the village of Georgeham above Putsborough Beach. His elm-plank writing hut still stands in a field at Ox's Cross; inside, it looks as if he has just stepped out for a walk on Baggy Point (his boots are against the wall, his desk ready for writing and his jacket still hangs on the back of the chair; to see it, you must join the Henry Williamson society, *see p55*). Williamson's grave is found in Georgeham churchyard. Tarka fans can trace the sites mentioned in the book along the 32-mile Tarka cycle trail from Barnstaple to Torrington.

For beachier escapades, families can forage for their supper. At low tide, people fish for prawns, which lurk in rock pools underneath clumps of bladderwrack seaweed. Pick up a prawning net from a local fishing shop, put on some old shoes and tie a plastic bag to your waist. Depending on the tides, the results can either be impressive (a big heaving bag of translucent prawns flicking ticklishly inside the plastic) or non-existent.

If you come up short, satisfy your cravings for a prawn sandwich at Mortehoe Shellfish restaurant. Or try again later. Like its powerful tides, this huge beach keeps pulling you back.

OTHER BEACHES

In the rush to get further west, North Devon is often overlooked by travellers. This is their loss. Some of the West Country's best beaches are found in this sleepy corner of the world, with the added bonus of Exmoor just inland. The beaches of Woolacombe,

Puttsborough, Croyde and Westward Ho! all offer waves and great expanses of sand. Croyde is one of Britain's top surfing beaches, backed by a pretty village of thatched cottages packed with surf shops. Woolacombe is arguably Devon's most beautiful beach, but it sports a busier, and more downmarket coastal strip of cafés and restaurants. Putsborough, meanwhile, offers a quieter family scene. Across the estuary Westward Ho!, has another sweeping stretch with more waves (it's a great beach for learning to surf) backed by a distinctive pebble ridge.

WHERE TO STAY AND EAT

The Saunton Sands Hotel (01271 890212, www.sauntonsands.com) may be a four-star operation, but glitzy it ain't. Still, there are fab sea views, two pools (one indoor) and it's good for families: there are decent crèches and luxury apartments too. Its minimalist Sands Café (01271 891288) serves coffee and light lunches all day, bistro food by night.

Atlantis Lodge (01271 890384, www.atlantislodge.co.uk) boasts five-star views and budget prices. Once a private house, it is now popular with surfers who use Croyde beach.

Wisteria and vines cover Combas Farm (01271 890398, www.combasfarm.co.uk), a 17th-century farmhouse B&B near Croyde. Comfortable rooms and breakfast with home-made jams and yoghurt complete the cottagey appeal. It's a short walk to Putsborough Beach, Baggy Point and Croyde Village.

North Morte Farm (01271 870381, www.northmortefarm.co.uk), near rugged Rockham beach, regularly tops the list of the country's best campsites. Bookings are not accepted, so phone on the day to see if there are spaces. Or try Hidden Valley, on a wooded river at West Down, near Ilfracombe (01271 813837, www.hiddenvalleypark.com).

Surfers swear by Mitchum's Campsites (01271 814022, www.croydebay.co.uk), a well-run beach-front pitch close to the waves.

Devon's freshest seafood is found at Mortehoe Shellfish (01271 870633, www.mortehoeshellfish.co.uk), a gloriously eccentric restaurant run by a local fishing family. Visitors are guided inside by an arrow on a plastic lobster on the lawn; the interior resembles a suburban front room. The menu is short and straightforward and makes the most of the freshly caught crab and lobster. The family also runs a shellfish van, which tours local campsites selling crab, lobster, cockles, mussels, whelks, prawns, crevettes and fish stuffed with herbs and wrapped in foil – ready for the barbecue. To get to the restaurant, follow the signs out of Barnstaple towards Woolacombe and Ilfracombe on the A361, then turn off at the B3343 for Mortehoe.

In Braunton, Squires Fish Restaurant and Takeaway (01271 815533) serves top-quality fish and chips; the frequent queues speak volumes. Further afield, Appledore offers picturesque narrow streets and another excellent chippie, up an alley beside the Seagate pub near the seafront. Hockings, the local ice-cream, is a Devon delicacy; it's manufactured in Appledore and available from vans at Westward Ho!, Instow and Ilfracombe. Their superlative vanilla ice-cream has a creamy, slightly salty taste like no other.

The local foodie mecca is 11 The Quay (01271 868090, www.11thequay.com), a Damien Hirst-owned restaurant in Ilfracombe. The views from the Atlantic dining room are worth the drive, as are the local oysters.

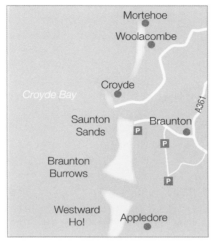

HOW TO GET THERE

By car Heading south on the M5, pass Taunton and exit at junction 27, followed by the A361 to Barnstaple, and then the B3231 to Braunton, Saunton Sands and the Burrows. You can walk to the Burrows from Saunton Sands, but for easier access take the B3231 signposted to Velator Quays as you come into Braunton, and then the toll road to Crow Point. **By train** To Barnstaple and then bus. **By bus** From Barnstaple bus station, take route 308 to Saunton Sands (Mon-Sat; Stagecoach Devon, 01392 427711, www.stagecoach bus.com).

PARKING

Pay parking at Saunton Sands, Croyde, Putsborough, Woolacombe and Westward Ho! For Braunton Burrows, park at Broadsands car park and follow the boardwalk through the dunes towards Crow Point. There is another car park (Sandy Lanes) on the Braunton-to-Croyde road.

FACILITIES

Beach huts (£12 daily, £70 weekly; contact Julian Humphries, 01271 890033, 07813 506899). Café. Shop. Toilets (disabled).

SPORTS

Cycling (Otter Cycle Hire, The Old Pottery, Braunston, 01271 813339; Tarka Trail Cycle Hire, Railway Station, Barnstaple, 01271 324202, www.tarkatrail.co.uk). Sand go-karting. Surfing (boards and pedal-powered go-karts both available for hire at Saunton car park; see also Saunton Sands Surf Lifesaving Club, www.sauntonsandssurflife savingclub.co.uk).

SWIMMING

Safe on Saunton Sands but avoid swimming near estuaries. Dangerous at Braunton Burrows (undertow). Beach patrols. Lifeguard in summer. Water quality: MCS recommended.

RULES

Dogs permitted in certain areas (signs). No barbecues, camping.

FURTHER REFERENCE

Braunton Tourist Information Centre (01271 816400, www.brauntontic. co.uk). Barnstaple Tourist Information Centre (01271 375000, www.stay northdevon.co.uk). Discover Devon (0870 608 5531, www.discover. devon.co.uk). Henry Williamson Society (www.henrywilliamson.co.uk). Local council (01271 327711, www.northdevon.gov.uk).

Thurlestone Sands

Mild at heart.

'Above all, avoid the moor, where the powers of evil are exalted.' So go the cautionary words of Sherlock Holmes to Dr Watson in *The Hound of the Baskervilles*. And anyone caught on Dartmoor on a damp, misty winter's afternoon, as the light fades and the chill seeps through your clothes, will know exactly what the sleuth was getting at. But just a few miles away, in a sleepy corner of South Devon, there is a stretch of coastline where the powers of evil assume no greater reality than a conceit in a novel. A place of such timeless repose, and such blissful tranquillity, that the noise of a car's engine is about as close to evil as you'll get.

Welcome to Thurlestone Sands, the beach that time did not so much forget as preserve in a beguiling cocoon of 1920s' modesty and restraint. Even the sea seems genteel, lapping gently away. Granted, the odd south-westerly swell can produce some ferocious surf, but in Thurlestone – so far removed from bustling modern life – even a storm can seem benign.

It is easy to imagine Turner here, 200 years ago, painting Thurlestone Rock (the natural arch, standing offshore, gives the town its name: Thurlestone, in Saxon, is a 'thirled' or pierced stone). Little seems to have changed since the artist's visit. South Milton Sands, Thurlestone's largest and most popular beach, is backed by lush and undulant fields and nature reserves (National Trust), which host a number of migratory birds; Leasfoot, a smaller shingle beach to the north-west over a headland, is similarly unspoiled. The sole concession to commercialisation is the South Milton café, which is more of a shack than a coffee-house. It's antiquated, but then, so is Thurlestone Sands.

The nearby, eponymous village was mentioned in a Saxon charter of 845, and the village church makes an appearance, in 1068, in the Domesday Book. Venerable historical provenance is not, though, the secret of Thurlestone's allure. Neither is golden sand; thanks to the endemic red sandstone of South Devon, the beach has a coarse feel and reddish hue. Nor are there oodles of activities for the kids: here, modernity gets as far as a bucket and spade.

But leaving the modern world behind is, of course, the reason to come to this part of Devon, on the tip of the South Hams. Time cannot but slow down when you start to navigate a series of winding lanes, often single track, with high hedgerows. If you don't like changing gears, Thurlestone will exasperate you, but this remoteness is part of its appeal. In the village there are thatched cottages galore and a sense of gentility more readily associated with the Cotswolds than the South-west. Refreshment in the Village Inn comes with a slice of history: some of its timbers were hauled from the wreck of the Spanish Armada vessel, the *San Pedro el Major*. In fact, Thurlestone had a starring role in the defeat of the Spanish Armada: it was in the turret of the village's 13th-century church that the first beacon fire was lit when the Armada was sighted.

Today, the bellicose is hard to imagine on this mild-mannered beach. In summer, the clear waters offer barely a ripple, making for excellent snorkelling and diving (there are some 30 wrecks in the area). The calm conditions in July and August do not, however, make for exciting surfing and windsurfing.

Still, you don't come here to test your physical limits. This is not the place to muse on the fragility of mankind in the face of a monstrous swell. No, Thurlestone evokes old-fashioned summer holidays – lazy days and a simpler time. You come here to idle, to read, to relax and to conjure adventure from rock pools.

There is a touch of glamour, however, and it is provided by the art deco Burgh Island Hotel, the retreat of early 20th-century names such as Agatha Christie, Noel Coward and Wallis Simpson. Visible from the eastern end of Thurlestone Sands, the sleek steel and concrete hotel resembles a stylish ocean liner. Built in 1927 and now Grade II-listed, it's the type of place where guests still dress for dinner. It is accessible by foot at low tide across a glistening stretch of sand. If flappers, the Roaring Twenties and Agatha

Christie murder mysteries float your boat (*And Then There Were None* and *Evil Under the Sun* were set here), Burgh Island calls for a splurge.

Back in Thurlestone, the most action you'll find is a bit of a breeze, and the right conditions to learn a new water sport. Chances are, though, that you'll end up staring at a becalmed sea, one that suggests nothing more taxing than a swim, or paddling a canoe, or taking a stroll along the coast path to Hope Cove. There, in a former fishing village etched into the walls of a green valley, are thatched cottages, and two sheltered sandy beaches with exceptional water quality; visiting seals and dolphins add to the sweetness. Above them, the tiny St Clement's Church completes the charming picture.

You don't have to be religious, however, to conclude that, in this part of the world, the powers of evil are far from exalted (Agatha Christie novels notwithstanding). If Sherlock Holmes had any sense, he would have quit Dartmoor and taken a break at Thurlestone.

Old-fashioned summer holidays – bracing dips and rock pool forays – still exist here.

OTHER BEACHES

There are quiet, secluded beaches at Hope Cove. Though five miles south of Thurlestone, it is an easy walk. Bantham, to the north, is much closer and combines a peaceful, get-away-from-it-all haven with the best surfing beach in South Devon. There can be good surf here even in the summer, with long waves breaking over the sandbanks near the rivermouth and in the middle of the bay. The Discovery Surf School (07813 639622, www.discoverysurf.com) is open all year round, offering lessons at Bigbury Bay.

Burgh Island, across the bay, was bought in 1927 by eccentric millionaire Archibald Nettlefold, who built an art deco hotel here. At low tide, a wide sandy beach emerges, bridging the island to the mainland. There is water on either side and lifeguards in summer. But be warned: to get there you have to make a lengthy drive inland to Bigbury-on-Sea in order to circumnavigate the River Avon. At Bigbury, you can park your car and walk across or take the Sea Tractor, a high vehicle that travels through shallow sea water and carries passengers on a platform. Back on the mainland, with views of the island, Challaborough is a sandy cove, which occasionally offers good surfing conditions.

WHERE TO STAY AND EAT

Time really does stand still at the Thurlestone Hotel (01548 560382, www.thurlestone. co.uk), owned and run by the same family since 1896. An upmarket country house hotel, it boasts an array of diversions: a golf course, a spa, two swimming pools, squash courts, snooker, sun terraces and, in keeping with the area's nostalgic ambience, a croquet lawn. For sustenance, the hotel's Margaret Amelia restaurant serves superb food – the choice between grilled fillet of john dory and a roast rib of Devonshire beef is a tough one. Needless to say, Devon cream teas are a speciality; the sea views are another reason to come. The Village Inn, part of the same hotel, is more down to earth. It serves well-kept ales and fresh seafood meals.

On a country lane in a 14th-century coaching inn, the Sloop Inn (01548 560489, www.sloopatbantham.co.uk) has character, and views of the countryside from its simple B&B rooms. Decent pub grub has a seafood slant. It's in the village of Bantham, a mile away from Thurlestone. Bantham's Village Store, on the hill, is an unexpected gem. The

store does a fine line in fresh coffee and tasty panini and baguette snacks; to the rear is a decked area with great views of Burgh Island and the brackish River Avon.

Splash out on the glamorous Burgh Island Hotel (01548 810514, www.burgh island.com) for the mysterious location, the architecture and the sheer retro fabulousness of it all. Note: full evening dress is required at dinner.

The Pilchard Inn (01548 810414), an old fishing cottage connected to the hotel, does pub meals for non-residents from Thursday to Saturday.

Kingsbridge, the area's principal town, boasts a number of restaurants and places to stay, and is an easy drive from Thurlestone.

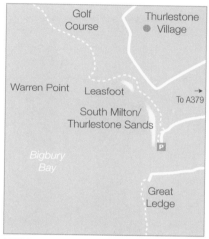

HOW TO GET THERE

By car From Totnes, in Devon, take the A381 towards Kingsbridge. After ten miles, turn right at a mini-roundabout on to the A379 towards Churchstow. At a second roundabout beyond Churchstow, turn left on to the B3197 then right into a lane signposted to Thurlestone. Follow the road to the sea. Access to Thurlestone Sands is mostly by single-track lane for the last 2.5 miles and is not good for disabled drivers. **By train** The nearest stations are Plymouth and Totnes. **By bus** Occasional bus service to Thurlestone and South Milton village (0845 600 1420, www.firstgroup.com).

PARKING
Pay (£3) but no disabled spaces.

FACILITIES
Café. Shops. Toilets at South Milton Sands.

SPORTS
Diving (Deep Blue Tech, 07791 152317, www.deepbluediving.org). Snorkelling. Surfing (Discovery Surf School, 07813 639622, www.discoverysurf.com). Wakeboarding and waterskiing (Shore Board Wakeboard and Waterski, 07967 989779). Windsurfing.

SWIMMING
Lifeguards (July-Sept). They start earlier, from May, at Challaborough and Bantham. RNLI service. Water quality: MCS recommended.

RULES
No camping. Barbecues and dogs are permitted (dog waste bins provided).

FURTHER REFERENCE
Kingsbridge Tourist Information Centre (01548 853195, www.kings bridge info.co.uk). Local council (www. southhams.gov.uk). Websites: www.thurlestonebeach.co.uk.

Slapton Sands

Beauty on the brink.

Contrary to its name, this is not a scrunch-your-toes in the sand sort of beach, but a vast shingle bar, stretching for three glorious miles along the South Devon coast, and distinguished by history, beauty, nature – and nakedness.

Vast it may be, but the bank is an intensely vulnerable place. The thin strip is bordered by water on both sides: a constantly encroaching sea, and an enormous freshwater lake. Despite its unique geography, not to mention gentle good looks, Slapton is not as famous as some of its Cornish and Devonian neighbours. But it has made headlines in the past, albeit for all the wrong reasons: its part in a hushed-up war-time tragedy; a village that was washed out to sea; and a series of storms that threatened to engulf the place. And it is well known to geologists, for its distinctive fragile shingle formation, which is similar to Chesil Beach. It is also cherished by naturalists (Slapton Ley, the inland lake, is a thriving reserve) and naturists (the area around Pilchard Cove, at the north end of the beach, is a mecca for nudists, which gives new – and comical – meaning to the name Slapton).

The masses, however, have largely stayed away. They may have been deterred by the narrow country lanes and the lack of sand. But the area's tranquillity has also been born of fragility; there has been little development here, as there may soon be trouble in paradise. The Slapton 'line' (as the shingle ridge is known) is being eaten away by the sea at an alarming rate. Back in 1917, the village of Hallsands (just south of the beach) was

washed out to sea during a winter storm, a sign of things to come. In 1947, the sea breached the beach and briefly joined the freshwater lake behind. More recently, seafront houses were severely damaged by storms in 1979; in 2001, 20 feet of the beach disappeared and part of the A379 was destroyed. Rising sea levels threaten the survival of the delicate freshwater ecosystem; soon, the Ley could become a saltwater marsh; more dramatically, the beach could be covered in shallow sea, as it was 3,000 years ago.

On a calm summer's day, however, Slapton's quiet beauty shows no sign of impending doom. A whiff of water mint scents the air, and the beach is splashed with the colours of gipsywart, iris and loosestrife. Walkers zigzag around the Ley, the largest freshwater lake in the south-west, or take in the views of Start Bay from the South West Coast Path. The nudists, including a sizeable gay contingent, strip off below the cliffs.

It may look cosy, but the village of Torcross is surrounded by water, and in danger of being engulfed.

Brave swimmers take a plunge (there is a steep drop and the water is cold). On a breezy day, windsurfers and kitesurfers blast across the bay. Fishermen snag bream, wrasse and pollack; porpoises and grey seals frolic in Start Bay and basking sharks can sometimes be spotted too. Water sports enthusiasts and sunbathers, meanwhile, gather at the seafront village of Torcross at the southern end.

Virtually surrounded by water, the village is perilously placed, but nonetheless the busiest stretch of the beach. In Tudor times, Torcross was merely a cluster of fishermen's stores – the fishermen themselves had the good sense to trade in sea views for safer living quarters inland. Today, the shops and holiday cottages huddle together at the water's edge, protected from the sea by a chest-high wall, built after a particularly ferocious storm. Despite its precarious location, Torcross oozes villagey English charm: cream teas, fish and chip shops and thatched cottages.

The cosiness is rudely interrupted by a Sherman tank, a monument to the 946 Allied soldiers who perished here during World War II. Back in 1944, the Americans were practising at Slapton for the D-Day landings. On the night of 27 April, a convoy of eight Allied Land Ship Tanks were destroyed by a German E-boat, a tragedy that was kept under wraps until the 1980s, when Ken Small, a local innkeeper, discovered old American coins and ammunition washed up on the beach and campaigned for a memorial; it stands on the Ley side, while another memorial was erected at the middle car park.

Despite the disaster, there is no lingering air of tragedy. On the contrary: every July, the place is positively buzzing for the annual Slapton Line Challenge, when mad locals race the length of the beach on foot and then paddle back by kayak.

Walking, though, is the most popular pastime at Slapton Sands, particularly around the Ley nature reserve, a haven for rare flora and fauna. Otter breed on the marshy banks, and migrant birds lure the twitchers. Binoculars poised, they come to ogle a seasonal cast

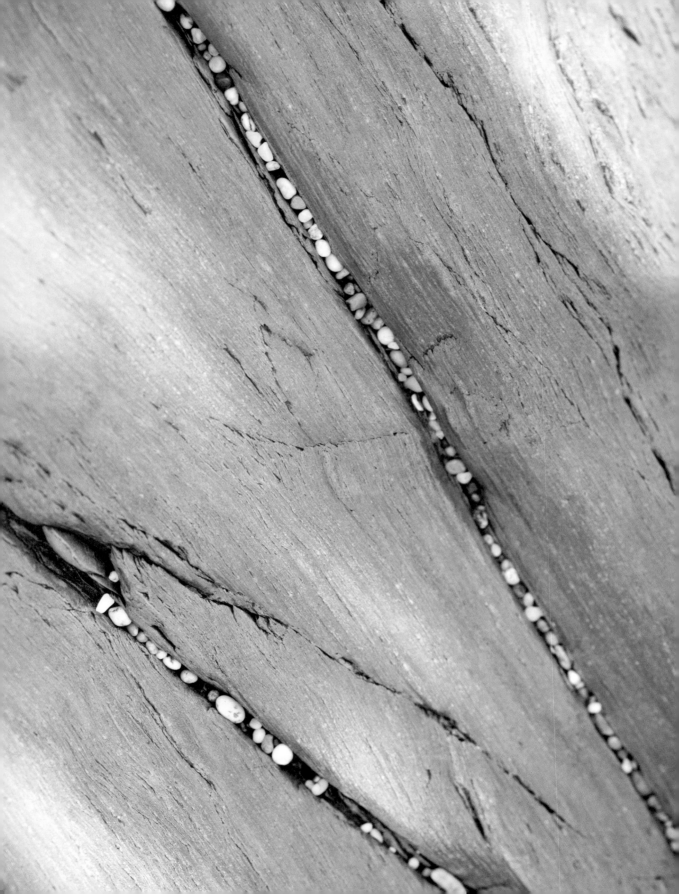

that includes the curlew and whimbrel in spring and autumn, warblers in the summer, ducks in winter, and cormorants, water rail and the rare great-crested grebe all year round.

The only signs of civilisation, apart from Torcross, are Slapton village (a haphazard inland hamlet comprising cottages, an ancient church and a field studies centre) and Strete. Reached by a steep incline from the northern end of the sands, the latter is distinguished by a classy string of cliff-top houses – and a magnificent vista. Here, there is a bird's-eye view of the beach; from above, its fragile position is laid bare. The war wounds have healed, but battles with mother nature are on the horizon.

OTHER BEACHES

Hallsands, south of Slapton, feels like a different world. The beauty takes on an eerie quality, when you consider that the village here was washed into the sea in 1917. You can view the remains from a platform near the Trout's Apartments at South Hallsands. North Hallsands, by contrast, still has an accessible beach, and is popular with a motley crew of nudists, fishermen and divers.

The closest place to find some real sand – albeit of a very coarse variety – is to the north, at neighbouring Blackpool Sands. A far cry from the famous Blackpool, it lacks donkeys, kitsch and rollercoasters. But it has beauty in abundance: it is a sheltered and unspoilt cove bordered by wooded cliffs and a subtropical garden oasis. Winner of a Blue Flag, it's more family friendly than its slap-happy neighbour, offering safe (and covered) bathing, an organic beach café, a shop and water sports equipment for hire.

If you're serious about water sports, and sand, go west. Bantham (see also p60) is renowned for its surfing and kitesurfing, and is backed by soft dunes.

Bucket and spades, rather than boards, are the norm at Bigbury-on-Sea. Another western neighbour of Slapton, it proudly waves its Blue Flag status on the other side of the River Avon, where it beckons you to build sandcastles and offers tantalising views of the exclusive Burgh Island (see p58).

WHERE TO STAY AND EAT

The shutters at Sea Breeze (01548 580697, www.seabreezebreaks.com) open on to the beach at Torcross, and the rooms are sprinkled with shells and driftwood. There's also a kitesurfing school and funky café on site, and bikes and kayaks are available for hire.

Winner of a Green Tourism Gold Award, Skerries B&B (01803 770775, www.skerriesbandb.co.uk) has eco credentials, a good location (on the cliff-tops) and a pleasing interior, with a terrace overlooking the sea and three comfortable rooms.

If you want your bed with some brews, the Tower Inn (01548 580216, www.thetowerinn.com) offers a handful of antiquated rooms and a good selection of real ales. The food and atmosphere are superlative. The menu comprises dishes from locally sourced ingredients, and the name derives from the setting, next to the remains of a chantry tower.

For a natural high, spend a night under canvas at Slapton Sands Camping and Caravanning Club Site (0845 130 7631, www.campingandcaravanningclub.co.uk), a well-equipped site with sea views and easy access to the beach.

For seafood, take a pew at the 14th-century Start Bay Inn (01548 580553, www.startbayinn.co.uk), and tuck into fresh crab sandwiches and locally landed fish, or take away a king-sized hunk of fish and sit on the beach.

Tucked away in Strete, the Laughing Monk (01803 770639) is considered a South Hams gem. Its West Country cooking has won multiple awards, and the ingredients are fresh and local (scallops, crab and lobster from Beesands, for instance). The characterful interior harks back to its former incarnation as a school, and the service is personal and personable.

The South West Coast Path offers a bird's-eye view of the beach and the Ley nature reserve.

HOW TO GET THERE

By car Slapton Sands is on the A379 between Kingsbridge and Dartmouth.
By train Slapton is not near any rail stations. Totnes is the closest, but you must take the 111 bus to Dartmouth, and then catch another bus from there (*see below*). **By bus** First Western National's 93 bus runs between Plymouth, Kingsbridge, Slapton and Dartmouth (there is one service per hour, 0845 600 1420, www.firstgroup.com; Traveline, 0870 608 2608, www.traveline.org.uk).

PARKING

Pay and display car parks by the beach at Torcross, Slapton Sands Memorial car park and Strete Gate. Overnight rates available.

FACILITIES

Cafés and pubs at Torcross. Ice-cream vans (seasonal). Toilets (disabled) at Slapton Sands Memorial, Strete Gate, Torcross. Slapton Ley Field Centre (01548 580466, www.field-studies-council.org).

SPORTS

Cycling and kayaking (for both, contact 01548 853524, www.endurancelife.com). Kitesurfing (Sea Breeze School, 01548 580697, www.seabreezebreaks.com).

SWIMMING

Safe swimming, but beware of steep drops in places. Lifeguards July-Sept. No lifeguard at Slapton Sands Memorial. Coastguard (999). RNLI lifeguard at Slapton Sands Torcross. Water quality: MCS recommended.

RULES

No camping. Barbecues permitted. Dogs permitted.

FURTHER REFERENCE

Kingsbridge Tourist Information Centre (01548 853195, www.kingsbridgeinfo. co.uk). Slapton Ley National Nature Reserve (www.slnnr.org.uk). Local council (01803 861234, www.southhams.gov.uk). Websites: www.barebritain.com; www. british-naturism.org.uk; www.sherman tank.co.uk; www.submerged.co.uk.

Chesil Beach

A natural wonder.

C hesil Beach is a romance, a mystery and a thriller, despite being perhaps best known to many from half-remembered geography lessons. A very rare type of 'tombolo' (or barrier spit), it is a coastal anomaly that disrupts comfortable notions of the seaside. If you crave a classic day at the beach – sand between your toes, a refreshing dip, seaside jollity – you've come to the wrong place. But if you are impressed by natural wonders and moody atmosphere (its momentous, otherworldly quality makes this the type of place where big decisions are settled), Chesil is oceans apart from the crowd. Indeed, what it lacks in pzazz, it makes up for in poetry. Seen from the Dorset hills above at night, it could be a great bank of cloud rising under the moon, with which it seems to share a natural affinity: pale, singular and lonely.

Locals call it Chesil Bank – a more appropriate moniker. It's a massive rampart of flint and chert pebbles, about 18 miles long, and visible from space. The beach is separated from the mainland by the Fleet, a shallow tidal lagoon that is a wetland of international importance.

But its geological credentials (it is 6,000 years old and the most southerly section of the World Heritage Jurassic Coast) garner the most attention. On the map, it looks as if some mad Neolithic Brunel had flung up a huge embankment of ballast to create a maritime motorway or sea railway from Bridport to Portland (calling at Nothing, Nowhere, and Emptiness). The mysterious air fits the geology. Experts have yet to agree on a satisfactory explanation for the origin of the thing: Ice Age landslips, rising sea levels and long shore drift are all supposed to have played a part.

It's not just geologists who are bewitched: the rich atmosphere has inspired authors too. Most famously, it was the setting for *Moonfleet*, J Meade Faulkner's Victorian smuggling adventure. More recently, the beach was employed to sly literary effect in Ian McEwan's *On Chesil Beach*, a poignant novella about an unconsummated honeymoon.

The melancholy air is not the figment of a romantic imagination. Dead Man's Bay, at the east end, has claimed countless lives from shipwrecks down the centuries, as vessels foundered here after being driven across Lyme Bay by relentless south-westerlies.

Indeed, Chesil has a terrifying undertow, with deep waves pounding and sucking remorselessly at the pith of the embankment. Not a top spot for sea bathing then, though it is a favourite with wreck divers.

Nor is it a particular favourite with walkers. A simple stroll can be an ordeal, demanding arduous, crunching, calf-punishing steps towards infinite space. What's more, the majority of the beach (between the Visitor Centre and Abbotsbury) is closed from May to the end of August to protect nesting birds. Beachcombers are similarly out of luck: pilfering of the pebbles is strictly prohibited (garden designers, be warned). The pebbles

are nevertheless an interesting spectacle: they have been graded in size by currents along the length of the beach, from fine gravel at West Bay to great big cobbles in the east near Portland. By sizing up a pebble, fishermen and smugglers could get a fix on their position along the beach in the dark. The former still come out in droves, casting from the shore in search of mackerel, garfish and plaice.

Despite the lack of traditional beachy pleasures, Chesil is more than just a mood piece. In the summer, sunbathers spread out along the stones. And at the west end of the Fleet, there is Abbotsbury. This picturesque 16th-century village is notable for cream teas, subtropical gardens, the romantic ruins of a Benedictine abbey and a medieval Tithe Barn (now a children's farm).

Its biggest claim to fame, however, is the Abbotsbury Swannery, the only sanctuary of its kind in the world. Founded in 1040 by Benedictine monks, who bred swans to eat at banquets, it is still going strong. The colony of 600 mute swans nests in the eelgrass beds of the brackish Fleet, and visitors can wend their way through the marshy haven. From March to May, it is nesting and egg-laying season; from mid May to late June, cygnets hatch from eggs in nests near the pathways.

A geological wonder, the shingle beach is 18 miles long, visible from space and backed by a tidal lagoon.

Similarly dreamy, Abbotsbury Subtropical Gardens cover 20 acres of a sheltered valley with camellias, magnolias and hydrangeas, amid many other rare and exotic plants.

To the east is the Isle of Portland. Formerly a naval base, this limestone outcrop is better known for its quarries, which produce the famous building stone. Portland Harbour will also enter the limelight when it hosts the sailing event at the 2012 Olympics. From breezy Portland Bill, the rocky southern promontory, the lighthouse museum and café provide a perch for watching the Fastnet Sea Race, a biennial event, in which yachts race past the dreaded peninsula. The treacherous currents are as challenging as any Hebridean whirlpool. Portland Bill also provides an iconic shot of Chesil Beach.

But the best view is back in Abbotsbury, at St Catherine's Chapel, a medieval gem that overlooks the beach. The building is dedicated to the patron saint of single women over 25, which brings us back to Ian McEwan's unhappy lovers, Edward and Florence. Though the novelist adds a postscript to the effect that the 'Georgian inn' where they share their excruciating wedding night in July 1962 is purely imaginary, he places it with some precision: 'just over a mile south of Abbotsbury, Dorset, occupying an elevated position in a field behind the beach car park.'

For those who have read the novel, these green empty fields above Chesil Beach will be a sad reminder of all things left unsaid or undone, chiming perhaps with the closing thoughts of Meade Faulkner's 15-year-old orphan hero, John Trenchard, on the beach: 'Yet I love to see it best when it is lashed to madness in the autumn gale, and to hear the grinding roar and churn of the pebbles like a great organ playing all the night. 'Tis then I turn in bed and thank God, more from the heart, perhaps, than any other living man, that I am not fighting for my life on Moonfleet Beach.'

OTHER BEACHES

Geologically speaking, Weymouth has Chesil Beach to thank for its existence, but the former has become the area's main seaside resort. George III popularised sea bathing here (his statue surveys the holiday throng), and the tradition continues, with a fine sandy beach and jolly seaside prom. On the Isle of Portland there are two 'raised beaches' (rock platforms that once touched the shore) and Church Ope Cove, a secluded spot below the ruins of Rufus Castle, supposed to have been built by the redbearded Norman king. Beyond Abbotsbury, heading west around Lyme Bay, the sea can be reached at a series of villages of varying charm, West Bexington perhaps the prettiest. West Bay, with its dramatic cliffs, shingle beach and fishing trips from the harbour, is very atmospheric. Further west, on the way to Lyme Regis, Seatown has a wonderful little sandy beach in the shadow of Golden Cap, the highest point on the south coast of England. The beach is overlooked by the convivial Anchor Inn and is a popular spot with fossil hunters.

Famous for its limestone, used in buildings around the world, Portland is also a rugged beauty spot.

WHERE TO STAY AND EAT

Moonfleet Manor (01305 786948, www.moonfleetmanorhotel.co.uk) is an 18th-century house right on the Fleet, though it seems to have been built facing the wrong way. Very shabby genteel, with some questionable artworks on the walls, it's nevertheless very family-friendly, with a huge games room for rainy days, and a trampoline and climbing frame for letting off steam. It has two restaurants and usually needs booking ahead.

In the heart of Abbotsbury, Ilchester Arms (01935 840220, www.ilchesterarms.com) is an old, stone coaching inn with ten rooms. Decent food is served in the friendly old bar, made cosier by log fires in the winter.

For camping, try Pebble Bank Caravan Park (01305 774844, www.pebblebank. co.uk), Sea Barn Farm (01305 782218, www.seabarnfarm.co.uk) or West Fleet Farm (01305 782218, www.westfleetholidays.co.uk).

The bright and airy Riverside Restaurant (01308 422011, http://thefishrestaurant-westbay.co.uk) is a local favourite, known for its expert way with fresh fish and its fine river views. Though it gets very busy, staff cope with aplomb. Booking is advisable.

The Pulpit Inn (01305 821237) at Portland Bill is a pleasingly old-fashioned boozer, serving up fresh seafood with sea views and the melancholy soundtrack of the lighthouse

foghorn. It also has cheap rooms. Also on Portland Bill, try the Lobster Pot café (01305 820242). A wooden bungalow with veranda, it is a great daytime option (it is open until 5pm) and close to the sea. Expect reasonably priced café meals, including fish.

The old Colonial Teahouse (01305 871732, www.abbotsbury.co.uk) in Abbotsbury Subtropical Gardens offers cakes and tea in a charming setting.

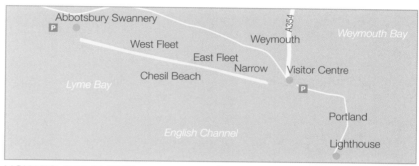

HOW TO GET THERE

By car From Dorchester, take the A354 (Roman Road) south towards Weymouth. For Abbotsbury, turn right at Elwell and head for Upwey, from where a minor road goes west to the B3157 coast road leading into the village. To get to Portland, follow the A354 south as far as it goes. At Ferrybridge, the road passes the Chesil Beach Visitor Centre. **By train** Weymouth. **By bus** Buses run from Weymouth (station) along the B3157 to Abbotsbury and on to Portland. First Hampshire and Dorset (02380 584321, www.firstgroup.com) and Sureline (01305 823039, www.sure linebuses.co.uk) operate services around here.

PARKING

Pay and display at Abbotsbury and the Chesil Beach Visitor Centre.

FACILITIES

Café (Abbotsbury). Toilets. Visitor Centre (01305 760579, www.chesilbeach.org).

SPORTS

Diving. Fishing (for both sports, contact West Bay Watersports, 01308 421 800; for deep sea fishing, contact Channel Warrior, 01460 242678, www.deepsea.co.uk). Kitesurfing.

SWIMMING

Strong undertow, not advisable. Water quality: not MCS tested.

RULES

No barbecues, bonfires, dune buggies, mountain bikes, pebble collecting. No camping on Portland. No walking on beach between Visitor Centre and Abbotsbury 1 May-31 Aug. Dogs permitted, except in the Fleet.

FURTHER REFERENCE

Tourist information (01305 251010, www.chesilbeach.org, www.westdorset. com). Abbotsbury Swannery (01305 871858, http://abbotsburytourism.co. uk). Local council (01305 838000, www.weymouth.gov.uk).

The Abbotsbury Swannery, home to 600 mute swans, is the only sanctuary of its kind in the world.

Durdle Door

The golden arch.

Danger is the last thing one would normally associate with Durdle Door, one of Dorset's most cherished beauty spots. Yet the road signs between the pretty, thatched-cottage villages of East and West Lulworth indicate that you should be prepared to risk life and limb to reach Durdle Door. 'Sudden Fire' reads one, while another warns drivers not of deer and tractors, but of tanks crossing. It adds up to a totally unexpected 'Basra moment' in this balmy corner of the country, where the MoD has kept a swath of army ranges since 1916.

Once you actually get there, Durdle Door is as safe as houses, apart from the steep steps leading down to the beach, or the odd tombstoner leaping madly off the arch. The dinosaurs that stomped this stretch of the Jurassic Coast have long since departed, leaving their 'footprints' in the fossil forest at nearby Lulworth Cove, while the seabirds that swoop over the chalky clifftops are harmless gulls, fulmars and kittiwakes.

The only danger, perhaps, is of being caught among the masses; the shingle beach here attracts thousands of visitors a year. They all come to stare at one thing: Durdle Door. The subject of a thousand postcards, this majestic natural arch has put this sleepy corner of Dorset firmly on the tourist map.

It first appeared on a proper map – the original edition of the Ordnance Survey map, to be specific – back in 1811. At the time, it was spelt Dirdale Door. (Silly names abound here: there's Scratchy Bottom, above Durdle Door, where the dividing lines of Bronze Age

field systems can be seen in the evening sunlight; and Bat's Head, a steep cliff beloved of birdwatchers, which juts out from the end of the beach.)

Soon after, it began to attract the attention of artists and writers. In 1819, John Keats was so bewitched by the place he wrote 'Bright Star, Would I Were Stedfast'. In 1874, Thomas Hardy wrote a memorable scene set in Lulworth Cove – renamed Lulstead – in *Far from the Madding Crowd*: in it, Sergeant Troy goes for a swim and is carried out by a current.

But the lesser-known Dorchester-born writer Llewelyn Powys (1884-1939) really captures the essence of the county's landscape in his *Dorset Essays* (1935). When the poet-philosopher wrote 'No sight is more provocative of awe than is the night sky', he might have been peering out to sea from a tent at the Durdle Door Holiday Park (Powys is commemorated by a stone along a public bridleway a mile west of Durdle Door).

Back then, Powys probably had these views to himself. Today, this stretch of coast is the most popular bit of the South West Coast Path, distinguished by grassy hills that tumble down to the edge of rugged chalky cliffs.

The perfect goblet-shaped bay of Lulworth Cove, sculpted by years of coastal erosion, mesmerises walkers. Yet it is the spectacular limestone arch of the eroding 'door', further west, that keeps them coming back. Geologists are similarly entranced by the spectacle. The arch was formed by the relentless pounding of the sea, which gradually punched a hole through the softer sections of rock (a smaller 'keyhole' arch is visible at the opposite end of the beach). Eventually, say the experts, the whole thing will collapse, leaving a sea stack similar to those found at Ladram Bay in east Devon.

But it has already been immortalised in popular culture – perhaps most famously as the backdrop to a number of music videos (including Tears for Fears' 'Shout', and, ahem, Cliff Richard's 'Saviour's Day'), plus the 2005 film *Nanny McPhee*.

Man O'War Bay, a sheltered cove to the east of Durdle Door, can be a respite from the crowds.

Such widespread exposure has ruined many a beauty spot before it. Not at Durdle Door. True, on a summer's day, a trail of walkers treads the path like ants. But the beach never gets insufferably crowded. For one thing, it's a mile's walk from the closest village (Lulworth Cove) across a hump-backed section of the South West Coast Path (and then there are those steep steps). For another, there are no facilities on the beach; toilets are an energetic hike up the hill, and the kiosk (for hot dogs, tea and whipped ice-cream) also requires a vertical climb.

What's more, beach snobs stay away, owing to the lack of pure sand (though Durdle Door's fine pebbles don't get in your eyes and are not bad for walking on). Still, it is often busy with bathers, even though there are no lifeguards, the shelf drops off suddenly and the water is cold (Man O'War Bay, a sheltered cove to the east of the Door, offers shallower seas). People who swim around the arch swear it is an ethereal experience – even more so when dolphins pay an occasional visit to the bay.

But landlubbers will not be unmoved either. Dorset has one of the most beautiful coastlines in Britain, and most walkers agree that the stretch from Worbarrow Bay to Osmington – which takes in Durdle Door and Lulworth Cove – is superlative. Gazing at the scene that spawned a thousand postcards, one soon forgets the nearby military base and hazardous road signs. The only battle you'll do here is with the beach brigade – and an army of photographers.

OTHER BEACHES

Lulworth Cove is more accessible than Durdle Door. The horseshoe beach is a slightly mucky mix of sand and large pebbles and is mostly overrun by the bucket-and-spade crowd. The cove is awash with dinghies and other small watercraft, but it's a safe enough space for kayaking and snorkelling. Handily, the Weymouth and Lulworth ferry service (Easter-Sept, 01305 833315) drops you at Durdle Door and other coves during the summer. For sustenance, there are a few tourist shops (Country Wines sells Lyme Bay liqueurs, pickles and Jack Ratt vintage cider) and a handful of hotels and restaurants. For rainy days, there is the 17th-century Lulworth Castle and a Heritage Centre (01929 400352, www.lulworth.com), which delves back to dinosaur days. The fossil forest – featuring the remains of trees from the Jurassic period – is just a short hike east of the cove.

The gently curved Ringstead Bay, between Lulworth and Weymouth, is not easily accessible, but there is plenty of space to spread out on the shingle and sand, with archetypal Dorset views of chalky cliffs and rambling farmland and fossils. Like many a great beauty spot, it has a nudist beach at its eastern end.

WHERE TO STAY AND EAT

The closest B&B to Durdle Door is West Down Farm (01929 400308, www.westdown farm.co.uk). Windswept and isolated at the top of a steep track, this remote farmhouse has an air of Hitchcock about it, with splendid views to match the atmosphere.

Gatton House (01929 400252, www.gattonhouse.co.uk), a turn-of-the-century mansion, combines English-stately-home schtick with fine views of the Purbeck hills. For a more casual alternative, try Breach House (07771 696591, www.lulworthcove.info) at

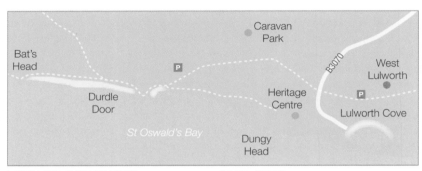

HOW TO GET THERE

By car From the M27 West, continue on the A31 to Bere Regis via Ringwood. At Bere Regis, follow signs to Wool, where you take the B3070 or B3071 from the main A352 to West Lulworth. After the village, turn right and follow signs to Durdle Door. **By train** Take any stopping train service for Poole, Dorchester and Weymouth and get off at Wool, where you can catch a 103 bus to West Lulworth. In good weather, take the train to Weymouth and catch the 9am ferry to Durdle Door returning at 5.30pm (Easter-Sept, 01305 833315). **By bus** Various services are offered. Call Nordcat Bus Services (0845 602 4547); Dorset County Council Passenger Transport (01305 225165); Linkrider (01305 834730).

PARKING

Pay and display at Durdle Door Holiday Park, a 15-minute walk from the beach, and Lulworth Cove, a 30-minute walk.

FACILITIES

Kiosk on the hillside. Toilets (disabled) and shop are located at Durdle Door Holiday Park.

SPORTS

Fishing. Scuba diving. Snorkelling (for all sports, bring your own gear).

SWIMMING

Beach drops away quickly. No lifeguards or emergency facilities. Water quality: MCS recommended.

RULES

No barbecues or camping. Dogs permitted (but access may be restricted May-Sept).

FURTHER REFERENCE

Tourist information (01929 552740, www.purbeck.gov.uk). Local council: www.wareham-tc.gov.uk. Website: www.visitingpurbeck.co.uk.

The spectacular views have made this region the most popular stretch of the South West Coast Path.

Lulworth Cove. A thatched house with simple, contemporary rooms, it offers self-catering, tempting vistas and proximity to the nearby coastal path.

Within walking distance of the beach, Durdle Door Holiday Park (01929 400200, www.lulworth.com) has about 100 tent pitches and the best sea view going.

For food, the Beach Café, Lulworth (01929 400648, www.beachcafelulworth.com) is rough and ready, but it's got a bayside location and serves fresh local fish (such as mackerel) and salad for a fiver. Its weekend-only evening menu offers more fish and BYO; diners have been known to end the night dancing on the tables.

The nearby Cove Fish seafood shack (01929 400807) sells the daily catch dispensed with recipe tips, and £2 pots of brown shrimps, winkles and mussels plus condiments. The Weld Arms (01929 400211, www.weldarms.co.uk) in East Lulworth serves fairly priced, tasty pub food; local specials include crab and tomato stacks and Lyme Bay scallops, pan-fried with black pudding, as well as Dorset ales and cider.

For picnics, stock up on freshly baked bread, Dorset cheeses and own-made pork pies at Goldy's Farm Shop in West Holme (01929 556777, www.goldys.co.uk).

Studland

An all-rounder with postcard good looks.

Could this be Britain's perfect beach? Studland certainly ticks all the right sandy boxes. It's the textbook definition of a 'great escape': a desert island idyll, less than three hours from London, and a stone's throw, but worlds away, from Bournemouth's bucket-and-spade brigade. It's a natural wonder (its dunes and heathland are a veritable wild kingdom), but with a touch of culture (a posh National Trust café, no less). And it's a crowd-pleaser, but without the crowds: it lures dreamers, who come for its pure, unadulterated tranquillity, and a mix of nature lovers and naturists (the sensual beauty seems conducive to baring all), plus the odd family. Add to this postcard good looks, warm waters and a few creature comforts, and you've got a British beach to rival the cream of the Caribbean.

Studland's reputation is based on a combination of gentle beauty and its vast shoreline, but the landscape is immensely varied. The north shore, for instance, is deceptively cosy. Tucked neatly into Shell Bay, it's a safe haven: Brownsea Island and the smart hotels of Sandbanks form a pleasing periphery; sailboats cruise in and out of Poole Harbour and the ferry (the prettiest way to approach Studland) cheerfully chugs back and forth. So far, so charming.

But once you round the corner, the vista changes dramatically. Knoll Beach, the east shore of Studland, is open season: wide, sweeping and exhilarating. Backed by grassy dunes, the three miles of pristine white sand are straight out of *Desert Island Discs*. People are conspicuous by their absence; the blue water has the requisite streaks of turquoise; the sandy bottom, sprinkled with the odd cockle, oyster and razorshell, slopes softly. In fact, swimming here is a picnic: in summer, the shallow waters are positively balmy and the surf kind. The sound of rustling grasses adds to the soothing scene.

And yet the gentle geography is punctuated by bursts of drama: the jagged limestone stacks of Old Harry's Rocks, say, or the majestic rolling hills of Ballard Down.

The most striking feature, though, is the eerie interior dunescape. Behind the grassy mounds where nudists build their sunbeds, the outlook is a carpet of greenery: heather, gorse, moss and lichen. A path meanders through the evocatively named brush (golden samphire, sea lavender and cat's ear). This otherworldly interior is frequented by bird watchers (who get their kicks from ringed plovers, curlews, oystercatchers) and body watchers (mostly gay men, who get their kicks from looking at each other). The former are in their element in the autumn, when thousands of waders descend on Studland to feed before flying off to Africa; the latter seem to show up any time, any season.

But the most ardent twitchers head further inland to Little Sea – a natural wonder. This freshwater lake was part of the sea until it became landlocked by the shifting dunes in 1880. Now it's the most crowded section of Studland, albeit with winged inhabitants: teal, mallard, little egrets, mute swans and herons and 20 different species of dragonfly.

Mother nature gives way to mothers and children at the southern tip of Knoll Beach, by the National Trust Visitor Centre, where the nudists cover up and the families let their hair down. Indeed, the area positively hums. In summer holidays, the sea here teems with (sporting) life: windsurfers, sailboats, canoes, banana boats, waterski boats, all hired from a kiosk. Families stake their claim in the sand with deckchairs and sunbeds. And the entire beach descends on Knoll Beach Café, which sums up Studland: a tasteful log cabin, with a noticeboard of butterfly sightings and a menu that serves paninis instead of hot dogs.

Ironically, though the busiest stretch of Studland, this is its least beautiful: the beach is narrower, the sand less pure and civilisation encroaches. And yet, even the beach huts at Studland are elegant: a string of painted green wood blending into a forest backdrop.

In stark contrast, Old Harry's Rocks stand out like a sore, if beautiful, thumb. These characterful, jagged chalk stacks underscore the area's geological interest: Studland marks the gateway to Dorset's Jurassic Coast, where rock fossils date back millions of years. They are the climax of a scenic path that veers through trees and clifftops, and reaches its zenith at a sublime lookout point – Dorset's answer to Beachy Head.

From the sublime to the respectable: behind Middle Beach lies the local metropolis: sleepy Studland village. Supposedly the inspiration for Toyland, the setting for Enid Blyton's *Noddy*, it still has a bourgeois 1950s vibe and a whiff of English nostalgia, although, apart from a Norman church and some thatched cottages, the architecture is more suburban than chocolate box. But its leafy surroundings ensure Studland's natural spell is not broken. And, with the exception of a couple of beer gardens, or a visit to the stables (you can go riding on the beach on summer evenings or in the winter), there's no reason to linger here. So once you've quenched your thirst and armed yourself with provisions, it's back to the beach, Studland's raison d'etre, and the desert island fantasy.

A crowd-pleaser without the crowds, Studland draws sports enthusiasts, nature lovers and families.

OTHER BEACHES

Bournemouth, just to the north of the Isle of Purbeck, is Studland's city cousin. The raw materials are the same: miles of immaculate white sand and safe swimming. But the ambience provides a sea change. By the pier, it's vintage seaside kitsch: a heaving

promenade, arcade games, sweet shops and an aquarium. North of the pier, it's blue rinse territory, with a string of sleepy seaside hotels. Dotted along this coast, there are a slew of more secluded beaches: Flaghead, Middle, Alum and Branksome Chines. All are reached via romantic, hilly wooded paths (chines, in old English) that lead to the beach. Leafy, quiet Branksome Chine is the loveliest. To the north, Boscombe will soon draw wave-riders, following the construction of an artificial surf reef offshore.

Sandbanks beach, south of the Bournemouth strand, is a big star in this area. Literally across the water, it is Studland's flashy sister, sprinkled with upmarket hotels, mansions and billionaire boat people. It boasts similarly sparkling sands, though it gets rammed.

Swanage, south of Studland, is a vintage family resort. It has a striking harbour, a long and fine sandy beach – recently shored up by rows of groynes – and clifftop walks galore, plus more Enid Blyton connections (she summered and wrote many of her books around here). Once a fishing village, it came of age as a seaside resort in Victorian times, and still retains a pier from that period, plus a diving school (there are lots of shipwrecks in the area) and a bustling lifeboat station.

In keeping with Studland's natural vibe, the beach huts blend into the woods.

WHERE TO STAY AND EAT

Manor House Hotel (01929 450288, www.themanorhousehotel.com) is a curious mix of olde worlde Englishness – 18th-century mansion, stately gardens, village location – and laid-back seaside resort (sunburnt beachgoers seek refuge here for tea or lunch). Inside, it's all oak panels and four-poster beds, but the sea views inject a breezy holiday vibe.

Knoll House Hotel (01929 450450, www.knollhouse.co.uk) looks more Cape Cod than coastal England. It's a low, sprawling gabled house set amid manicured lawns and tennis courts, high on a hill overlooking the sea. The plain bedrooms won't make it into the pages of *Wallpaper** any time soon, but the lush grounds and pool-with-a-view provide the eye candy.

The Bankes Arms Country Inn (01929 450225, www.bankesarms.com), an ivy-covered pub in Studland village, contains ten bedrooms and a scenic beer garden. It's also a good choice of restaurant: with its log fires and candlelight, it's relentlessly cosy, and has a good reputation for seafood. But its real claim to fame is beer: real ale connoisseurs come from far and wide.

The Shell Bay Seafood Restaurant and Bar (01929 450363, www.shellbay.net), has a bright and breezy setting (the edge of Poole harbour) and a fresh seafood menu. The tasteful Knoll Beach Café (01929 450305, www.purbeck.gov.uk), in the National Trust Visitor Centre, is a far cry from candy floss and hot dogs. Expect local foodie fare: Bridport pork pies and paninis with cranberry Somerset brie. For classic beach junk food, there are more options — and less ambience — at the Middle Beach Café (01929 450411), further south. Next door, an ice-cream stand operates in the summer.

HOW TO GET THERE

By car From Poole, take the A3049 to Wareham, followed by the A351, then the B3351 to Studland village. Ferry Road runs north through to South Haven Point (the ferry docks). Alternatively, take the B3065 from Bournemouth to Sandbanks and catch the ferry to Studland. **By train** Wareham, Poole or Bournemouth rail station, then bus. **By bus** Services from Wareham to South Haven Point via Studland are provided by the Wilts and Dorset Bus Company (www.wdbus. co.uk). There are also buses from Poole and Bournemouth (01202 673555). Ferries (01929 450203, www.sandbanksferry.co.uk).

PARKING

Pay parking at South Haven Point, Knoll and South Beach, NT members free with card.

FACILITIES

Beach huts (01929 450259). Café (2). Deck chairs/sunbeds (07980 559143). Learning Centre (01929 477320). Pub. Restaurant. Shop. Toilets (nappy-changing facilities, disabled). Visitor Centre.

SPORTS

Banana boat rides and powerboat rides, until mid Sept. Canoeing. Kayaking. Sailing. Water bikes. Waterskiing. Windsurfing (for all water sports, contact 07980 559 143). Horse riding at Studland Stables (01929 450273, www.studlandstables.com).

SWIMMING

Shallow shelf, no undertow. Lifeguard. Beach ranger (07970 595963). Coast guard (01305 760439). Water quality: both Knoll Beach and Shell Beach are MCS recommended.

RULES

No dogs on Knoll or Middle Beach 30 June-2 Sept. No jet skis. Dogs permitted from 1 Oct–30 April; on leads from 1 May-29 June and 3-30 Sept. Fires and barbecues (designated areas only). Nude sunbathing permitted at Knoll Beach between signs.

FURTHER REFERENCE

National Trust Visitor Centre & Shop (01929 450500, www.nationaltrust.org.uk). Local council (01929 556561, www.purbeck.gov. uk). Website: www.worldheritagecoast.net.

West Wittering

A tale of two beaches.

With its gently shelving sands and shallow, sun-warmed tidal pools, West Wittering is a paradise for families. Sheltered by the Isle of Wight and the rolling swell of the South Downs, it enjoys its own benign microclimate, earning it the sobriquet 'God's pocket' among locals. Even on blustery days, there's a chance the sun will be shining down here – and if not, cups of hot chocolate from the beach café and old-fashioned British stoicism fortify the faithful and their wetsuit-clad offspring. Yet inviting as its clean sands and calm waters may be, that's only half the story. At the western end of the beach, East Head's shifting sand dunes and salt marshes possess a desolate, other-worldly beauty – a haven for wildlife and those in search of solitude.

The best way to get to the beach (and bypass the snaking queue for the car park on summer weekends) is to cycle down from Chichester on the Salterns Way Cycle Path. Eleven miles long, it runs past sleek, gleaming boats at Chichester Marina, across sun-dappled fields, along lily-covered waterways and through cool, dim copses before finally emerging in West Wittering village, a charming slice of nostalgia with its Sussex flint-studded cottages and tiny, peaceful church.

The sandy, Blue Flag beach is equally tranquil: no jagged cliffs or pounding breakers here. Bathers potter in the shallows at the edge of the sea: a vast, shimmering expanse, broken only by the white yacht sails that dot the Solent; further out, to the south-west, rises the green-grey outline of the Isle of Wight.

Thanks to a group of enterprising locals, who pooled resources and bought the beach and surrounding grassland in 1952 to save it from developers, the inland vista is equally idyllic. There are no crazy golf courses and amusement arcades to distract the kids from sandcastle-building; no naff bungalows and caravan parks to encroach on the landscape's pristine beauty. Instead, the wide, sloping sands are backed by a tall tamarisk hedge, a row of weathered beach huts and a 20-acre swathe of grassland, occupied by butterflies, picnicking families and pleasingly wonky lines of parked cars. Beyond, the gently undulating South Downs form a picture-perfect backdrop.

Simple pleasures are the order of the day here. At low tide, a quarter of a mile of fine, softly sloping sand emerges, along with shallow tidal pools and a sandbar-sheltered lagoon. Children paddle and drift on dinghies in the smaller pools. The bigger tidal lagoon, meanwhile, is perfect for a sedate swim, and a mecca for kitesurfers and windsurfers – its calm waters are ideal for showing off (the old hands) or falling off (the novices).

Aside from the windsurfing club, the beach's sole concession to commercialism is a low block housing a beach shop, café and takeaway hatches. Most beachgoers bring a picnic or spark up a barbecue: come midday, the heady smell of browning sausages wafts across the dunes, and sandcastles are momentarily forgotten.

At the western end of the beach, East Head, a lovely sand and shingle spit, marks the entrance to Chichester Harbour. On its seaward side, the sandy strand is narrower than the main beach, but infinitely quieter. Here, the sea deposits treasures: pearl-lined slipper limpet shells, razor clams, cockles and whelks.

The northernmost tip is the busiest spot, as passing yachts drop anchor for lunch and a dip, and day-trippers sprawl on the sand. Off-season, their place is taken by a colony of harper seals, who swim across from Thorney Island to bask in the winter sunshine and solitude. But even at the height of summer, there's peace and quiet to be found. Venture away from the shoreline, into the sand dunes, and you're suddenly in glorious isolation. Skylarks flit overhead, singing out warning of an intruder, while tiny lizards dart away, leaving narrow trails criss-crossing the sand.

Though it is completely unspoiled, this family-friendly beach is an easy day trip from London.

It's a disorientating, constantly evolving landscape: shaped by the wind and waves, the dunes are endlessly shifting, gathering around the clumps of spiky marram grass and forming and reforming into new patterns. Roped-off areas protect ringed plover nesting sites and dunes where rare silver spiny digger wasps burrow – one of the reasons this is a designated Site of Special Scientific Interest (SSSI), protected by the National Trust. Spread a picnic blanket amid the dunes and delicate sea bindweed flowers, and you could be the last person on earth – until an intrepid small child appears on the horizon, playing hide and seek.

On the landward side, salt marshes are bleakly beautiful at any time of year, and transformed in early summer into a meadow of purple sea lavender. Where East Head meets the mainland, a footpath meanders along the edge of the marshland and around the harbour to the sailing village of Itchenor. Along the way is the green triangle of Snow Hill Common and the diminutive, white-painted row of old coastguard's cottages, built to deter 18th-century smugglers, who used Snow Hill Creek to transport contraband. Here, too, is the crabbing pool, where small children (and competitive fathers) gaze with rapt attention into the murky depths, trying to entice its scuttling inhabitants with bacon-baited lines. At Itchenor, summer boat trips explore the harbour, and the footpath

stretches onwards to Chichester Marina and beyond. But the handsome, red-brick Ship Inn beckons, with its locally brewed real ales and gargantuan fish and chips.

With the day drawing to an end and small fry's bedtimes fast approaching, the beach at West Wittering slowly empties. Follow the footpath back, find a vantage point on the dunes and drink in the view. As the sun sets over the glittering Solent, God's pocket truly does seem blessed.

OTHER BEACHES

A few miles along the coast, towards the tip of the splendidly named Manhood Peninsula, is Bracklesham Bay. Surrounded by an unlovely sprawl of modern bungalows, the shingle-backed beach may not be as inviting as West Wittering – but there's fine fossil-hunting to be had here. Dark, sea-polished sharks' teeth and fossilised shells wash up regularly, with particularly rich pickings after stormy weather.

If West Wittering is resolutely uncommercial, Bognor Regis, just east, is a shameless people-pleaser. Its safe bathing and five-mile stretch of sand and shingle have been drawing the crowds for decades, though these days its modesty-protecting bathing

machines and genteel boarding houses have given way to a giddy whirl of seaside pleasures: amusements galore, chippies, a miniature train, trampolines and crazy golf.

A few miles to the east, a very different seascape awaits at Climping beach. Quiet and starkly beautiful, it's got next to nothing in the way of amenities. At low tide, the pebbles give way to a swathe of fine, dark sand, while the secluded dunes are home to rare plant species and wildlife (and the occasional gay cruiser).

The sea breezes and clear waters make West Wittering a mecca for water sports enthusiasts.

WHERE TO STAY AND EAT

In West Wittering village, the Beach House (01243 514800, www.beachhse.co.uk) is a bright and breezy B&B, with spacious rooms and genial staff. Claim a table on the wooden veranda and enjoy some sterling local seafood: Sussex smokies, whole tail scampi or beer-battered fish and chunky chips.

At nearby East Wittering, the Dodo (01730 814002, www.thedodo.co.uk) is a stylish slice of seaside living. Built around two converted railway carriages and gorgeously kitted out, it has been transformed into a house that sleeps 12. Outside, there's an old-fashioned bath for alfresco dips, and a wooden terrace with splendid sea views.

Camping options abound round these parts. Closest to the beach is Wick's Farm Holiday Park (01243 513116, www.wicksfarm.co.uk), winner of a Gold David Bellamy Conservation Award. In East Wittering, the grassy paddock at Stubcroft Farm (01243 671469, www.stubcroft.com) is another idyllic spot to set up camp. A haven for wildlife, the site is run on environmentally friendly lines – hence the waterless eco-loos. If the great outdoors gets all too much, there's a B&B in the Victorian farmhouse.

Perched by Pagham nature reserve, the Crab and Lobster (01243 641233, www. crab-lobster.co.uk) has a romantic setting and a polished, gastropub-style menu. It boasts four sleek bedrooms; the attic room has a telescope looking out across the marshes.

The Old House at Home (01243 511234, www.oldhousepub.co.uk) is West Wittering's only pub. Its menu offers hearty, own-made pub classics (sausage and mash, scampi and chips, game casserole) made with local produce.

Locals are unanimous that the best fish and chips on the peninsula are to be found at the Boathouse in East Wittering (01243 673386).

HOW TO GET THERE

By car From Chichester, take the A286 south for seven miles. In West Wittering, turn right after the row of shops: 500 yards on, a left-hand turn leads to the beach and car park. **By train** Chichester is the nearest rail station. **By bus** The 53 bus from Chichester goes direct to West Wittering; the 52 runs via Bracklesham (0845 121 0170, www.stagecoachbus. com/south). **By bicycle** Chichester is an 11-mile ride from the beach via the Salterns Way Cycle and Wheelchair Path (01243 775888, www.conservancy.co.uk/ out/cycling.asp)

PARKING

Pay parking.

FACILITIES

Café and shop Apr-Oct. Beach cleaners (summer). Bins. Child-safe band scheme. First-aid post May-Sept. Toilets (disabled, nappy-changing facilities). Showers.

SPORTS

Body boarding. Horse riding (01243 672194). Kite buggying (www.west witteringsbuggyclub.co.uk). Kitesurfing. Sailing (www.wwsc.co.uk). Surfing. Windsurfing (for water sports, contact Wittering Surf Shop, 01243 672292).

SWIMMING

No swimming flags. Lifeguards (May-Sept), but not at East Head. Water quality: West Wittering, Blue Flag. MCS approved. Quality Coast Approved. East Head not MCS tested.

RULES

No launching of motorised craft from beach. No horse riding 9am-6pm May-Sept. Barbecues and dogs permitted (restricted areas for dogs May-Sept).

FURTHER REFERENCE

Chichester Tourist Information Centre (01243 775888, www.visitchichester. org/tic). Local council (01243 785166, www.chichester.gov.uk). Website: www.westwitteringbeach.co.uk.

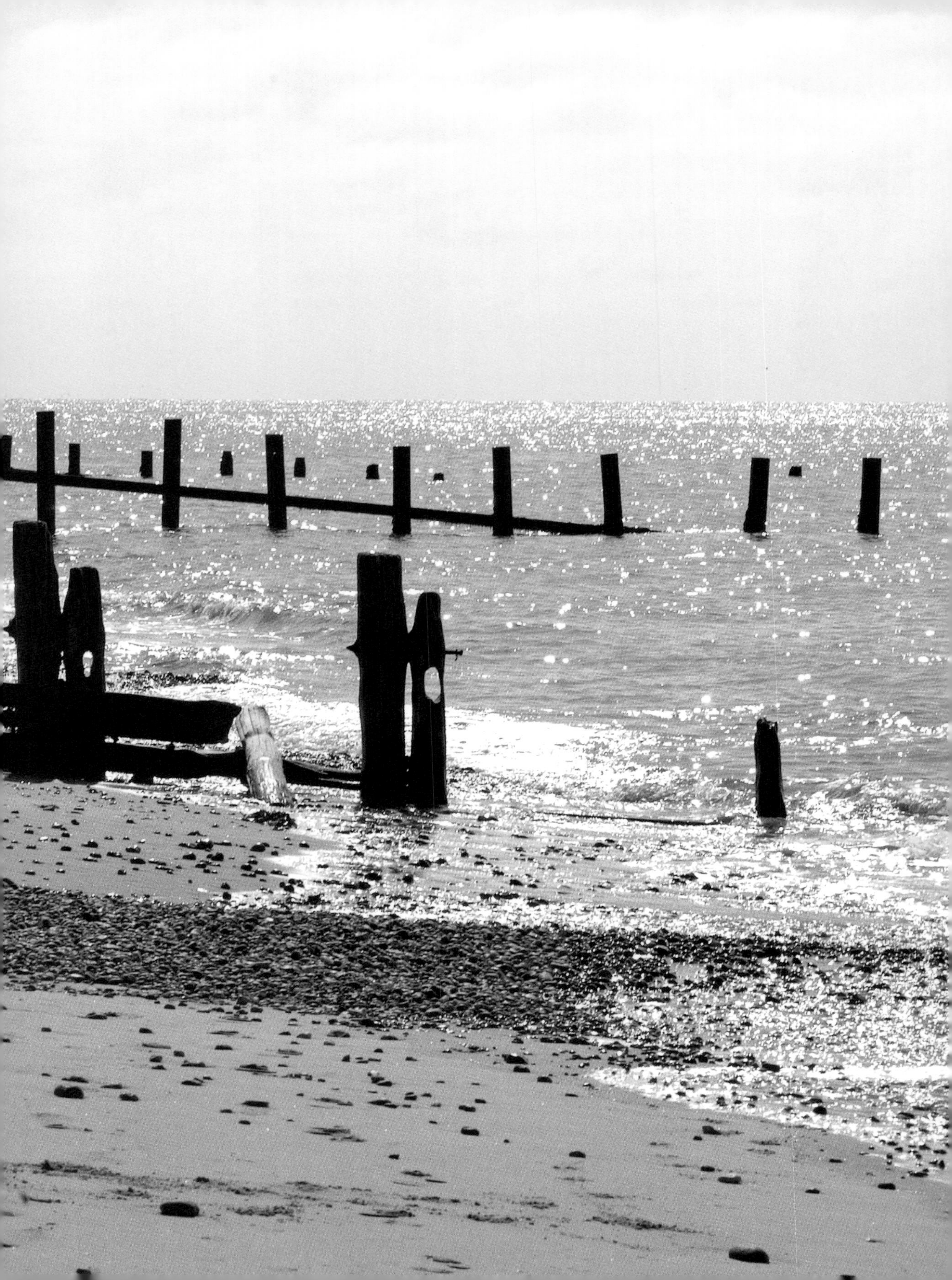

Camber Sands

Big, beautiful and born again.

We do, as the song goes, like to be beside the seaside, but let's face it: the anticipation is half the fun. There are beaches that spread out before you as you approach them, laying their features out like a market stallholder displaying sparkling gewgaws. There are beaches that tempt from a distance, coming into focus as you descend from the hills. And there are beaches that hide their majestic landscapes behind high dunes, rewarding you at the last minute with surprising views; sometimes leaden, slate-grey skies and black seas, sometimes crashing waves, sometimes the sea so far out that it's barely there and the sky stretching on forever, and sometimes – those perfect times – bright blue seas, glorious blue skies and golden sand.

Such a beach is Camber Sands, which withholds its beauty until the last second. Hidden behind a mountain of dunes, it is an awesome spectacle: a vast, windswept expanse of soft, sandy beach, seven miles long and, at low tide, a staggering half a mile wide. Situated west of Dungeness and east of Rye, Camber lacks the character of the former and the classiness of the latter, but, in terms of pure, unadulterated beach, this is arguably the best strand on the south coast.

Its immensity breeds versatility. Here are families hunkering down in their sturdy windbreak bunkers (you'll need them) and building huge sandcastles, or paddling and swimming in the clean seas. At the water's edge are couples walking dogs and riders gently cantering through the surf on horseback. Kiteboarders and windsurfers, for whom Camber is a huge destination, career across the sand and through the waves. Back in the dunes, nature-lovers watch the wildlife.

The sand dunes are an anomaly along the pebbly Sussex coast. No piddly little mounds these, but towering peaks and broad valleys that give you some idea of what walking in a desert must be like. In fact, the dunes have stood in for deserts in a number of film shoots – notably acting as the Sahara in the 1967 film *Carry On... Follow That Camel*. To act out your *Lawrence of Arabia* fantasies, walk away from the village to the west end of the beach. Here, the dunes are at their biggest and the sands are secluded.

Not only are the dunes rare for these parts, they're a Site of Special Scientific Interest. They host wildlife (hen harriers, short-eared owl and snow bunting all spend winters here) and have an interesting geological story to tell: they have gradually formed over the last 350 years and are growing by about 300,000 square feet every year. The mounds take shape when sand blows inland and builds up around plants and fences – in Camber's case, pretty, traditional chestnut fences, erected to help stabilise the dunes. Mother nature contributes too: marram grass, which fringes the beach, has a deep root system that holds the sand in place.

If not for these defences, both natural and man-made, the village of Camber would be swallowed up by the sea or buried under the sand. For some people, this wouldn't be such a bad thing. Bordered by a 3,000-capacity car park and a Pontins Holiday Camp, Camber village is not exactly synonymous with class in the popular imagination. In fact, it was once determinedly downmarket and downright unappealing.

But the area is subtly changing, particularly at the western end. Though the western car park has a nasty-looking café (think cheap burgers and plastic beach tat), it has recently been overshadowed by a spiffy new neighbour. In fact, the scene calls to mind a hoary old John Wayne in a frontier town, facing off the young brash sheriff across the road – in this case, the Place, a brasserie and boutique hotel. Here, good coffee and great food, once unheard of in these parts, have put Camber on the foodie map.

On the pebbly Sussex coast, the sands at Camber are greatly appreciated by barefoot explorers.

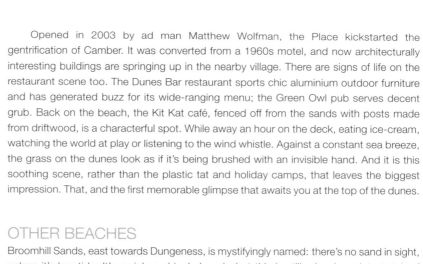

Opened in 2003 by ad man Matthew Wolfman, the Place kickstarted the gentrification of Camber. It was converted from a 1960s motel, and now architecturally interesting buildings are springing up in the nearby village. There are signs of life on the restaurant scene too. The Dunes Bar restaurant sports chic aluminium outdoor furniture and has generated buzz for its wide-ranging menu; the Green Owl pub serves decent grub. Back on the beach, the Kit Kat café, fenced off from the sands with posts made from driftwood, is a characterful spot. While away an hour on the deck, eating ice-cream, watching the world at play or listening to the wind whistle. Against a constant sea breeze, the grass on the dunes look as if it's being brushed with an invisible hand. And it is this soothing scene, rather than the plastic tat and holiday camps, that leaves the biggest impression. That, and the first memorable glimpse that awaits you at the top of the dunes.

OTHER BEACHES

Broomhill Sands, east towards Dungeness, is mystifyingly named: there's no sand in sight, unless it's low tide. It's mainly a shingle beach, but this is still a lovely, quiet stretch of coast. There's nothing here but sea, and the odd kite flyer or windsurfer (many of whom park here to avoid charges at Camber), but that's part of the appeal. Winchelsea Beach, a few miles west, is another shingle beach whose dilapidated groynes and mirror-like rock pools give it an ethereal beauty – great for long walks and atmospheric photographs, particularly at low tide. If the shingle proves too tricky, there's a promenade, so you can keep your eye on the sky without wobbling around on the ground. *See also pp112-119.*

WHERE TO STAY AND EAT

The Place at Camber Sands (01797 225057, www.theplacecambersands.co.uk) is a minimalist boutique hotel built around a courtyard, minutes from the best part of the beach. The brasserie has been garnering lots of press: it serves locally sourced produce

(including wines) and seafood from sustainably fished sources. The chic decor, all glass and blond wood, is the new face of Camber Sands.

In the heart of one of England's prettiest towns, the George in Rye (01797 222114, www.thegeorgeinrye.com) is an old coaching inn done up with modern luxuries, including flat-screen TVs, marble-top bathtubs and sumptuous bedlinens. There's a menu to match: ex-Moro chef Rod Grossmann cooks up a storm of adventurous modern English cuisine with exotic touches.

The Hope Anchor Hotel (01797 222216, www.thehopeanchor.co.uk), also in Rye, is small and charming. Built in the mid 18th century, it is filled with characterful antique furniture and even has the odd secret passage.

Back in Camber Sands, the Green Owl pub (01797 225284, www.thegreenowl.co.uk) has six simple, but cheerfully decorated bedrooms and serves decent pub grub.

Apart from the Place, welcome alternatives to caff food include the Dunes Bar and Restaurant (01797 224567), which tries to use local produce where possible. The menus change seasonally. In winter, there's an own-made steak pudding.

In Rye, the Fish Café (01797 222226, www.thefishcafe.com) serves some of the best seafood in the area, alongside a good choice of meat and vegetarian options.

There is always a breeze blowing at Camber Sands, so most visitors bring a windbreak or a kite.

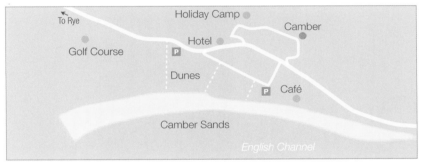

HOW TO GET THERE

By car From Ashford (M20) take the A2070 to Brenzett. Turn on to the A259 signposted New Romney/Hythe. Turn left on to B2075, signposted Lydd, from Lydd follow signs for Camber. From Hastings/Rye, take A259 towards Hythe, then B2075 three miles east of Rye. **By train** Nearest station Rye. **By bus** Hourly service from Rye to Camber/Lydd (08702 433711, www.stagecoachbus.com); every two hrs Sundays/ holidays.

PARKING

Pay and display. To avoid the crowds, choose the western car park.

FACILITIES

Beach inspectors. Cafés. Children's play area. Deckchairs (hire). Emergency phones (01797 225207). First aid post. Lost child centre. Shops. Slipway. Toilets (disabled). Windbreaks (hire).

SPORTS

Horse riding (for regulations, contact 01797 225207). Kiteboarding. Kitesurfing. Sailing. Waterskiing. Windsurfing (for info on water sports, call 01797 321885, www.actionwater sports.co.uk; 01797 225238, www.ryewatersports.co.uk).

SWIMMING

No lifeguards/coastguards. Water quality: MCS recommended. Quality Coast award.

RULES

No bonfires or barbecues. Dogs allowed (on leads) between zones F and H, May-Sept.

FURTHER REFERENCE

Tourist information: The Heritage Centre, Rye (01797 226696, www.visitrye.co.uk). Local council (01424 787878, www.rother.gov.uk).

Dungeness

A different light.

A picnic in the sand? A paddle in the shallows? Kiss me quick? Not here. Those classic British seaside pursuits are just not possible at Dungeness. This lonely strip of hard, unyielding shingle doesn't just look different to the average Kent beach – the entire promontory barely looks like England at all. The sky stretches high and wide over flat marshland; a scattering of fishing shacks looks small and vulnerable against the eerie, light-filled expanse; the steep pebbly banks (this is the largest expanse of shingle in Europe) are constantly reshaped by the relentless smash and pull of the sea.

And yet all this isolation and strangeness has its advantages: on fine days, when the English Channel turns a rich, deep blue, the beach remains sparsely populated, with none of the tumult and cheek-by-jowl compromise that accompany hundreds of families descending on one place. And when the weather's not so clement, Dungeness comes into its own, allowing you to believe – for a few hours – that you're the only person left on this cramped island, with only the roiling grey-green water and the low hum of Dungeness' power station for company.

In a landscape where there are many unusual features, the imposing hulk of a nuclear power plant is the most unexpected. There are two reactors: one built in the 1950s and decommissioned in 2007, the other built in the 1980s, and still generating electricity.

But the biggest danger to day-trippers is not a nuclear explosion – touch wood – but the treacherous waters. Indeed, the term 'water's edge' should be taken literally here. Where the shingle meets the sea, there is no gentle lapping and no possibility of cooling

The bleak landscape has its advantages: even on a sunny day, Dungeness is sparsely populated.

off up to the knee. Waves rise to the edge of the banks, smash down and then suck the shingle mercilessly, hissing in retreat. If paddling is hazardous, swimming would be suicide. After all, this beach was created by the power of longshore drift, which pushed shingle into banks up to 60 feet deep. The tide's strength has the opposite effect too, and a fleet of lorries is routinely deployed to shore up the stony piles and prevent them from being reclaimed by the sea.

No wonder anglers are a more common sight here than families. Apart from solitary walkers, Dungeness's bread and butter consists of those hoping to ensnare a fish. In fact, the same conditions that make for lousy swimming ensure wonderful fishing: thanks to the steep shelving, the water is so deep that it's possible to fish off the edge of beach just as you might from the banks of a deep reservoir. Just visible in the curling waves are whole schools of fish, silvery flashes darting along parallel to the coast. Local diehards eat the fish caught here, despite any possible deleterious effect from the power station's warm, chlorinated waste waters.

If dangerous to swimmers, and vital organs, the currents have historically been no more forgiving to boats; there is still an RNLI station here, with its immaculately polished lifeboat (and small museum) and the coast is littered with wrecks. Intricate maps framed in the Old Lighthouse pinpoint the lost vessels.

Built in 1904, this lighthouse is now defunct (there is a new, black-and-white striped one, built in 1961), but is still open to the public (you can even get married here). Squeeze yourself on to the viewing platform to really understand the lie of this odd land. From the

highest vantage point, dark railway tracks slash through the sparse and scrubby earth below; Dungeness is the end of the line – physically and spiritually – for the Romney, Hythe and Dymchurch Light Railway. From above, the bleakness of this landscape is magnified; featureless to the average eye, it soon becomes apparent why Dungeness has been deemed Britain's only desert, though the scene is more *Flintstones* than *Lawrence of Arabia*.

Bizarrely, the natural environment seems to have benefited from the industrial detritus (gravel pits, nuclear power station). Dungeness is a breeding ground for unusual and rare forms of flora and fauna. Blackthorn and sloe trees submit to the elements by keeping low, growing along the ground. Other plant life includes the sea pea, Nottingham catchfly, viper's bugloss and yellow-horned poppy. Fluttering above, the rare Sussex emerald moth appears in July. The old gravel pits harbour the protected great crested newt and the medicinal leech. Spiders are in their element too: there are 302 species, from the orb-weaver to the worryingly named spitting spider (arachnophobes beware).

Twitchers, on the other hand, will have a field day: there is an RSPB nature reserve with hides for viewing species such as the Slavonian grebe, the smew and bittern. Instead of driving away the birds, the power station seems to have done the opposite – the warm waste water has enriched the sea's biology and thus lured sea birds.

Not exactly Blue Flag material, then, but Dungeness has always been an acquired taste. Despite this, or perhaps because of it, this moody corner of Kent has never been short of fans, who have found a singular charm in its bleak ambience. The film director

Derek Jarman lived here, in Prospect Cottage, where his garden of beachcombings, driftwood and weirdly sculptural plants still draws curious visitors, years after his passing.

Jarman's experimental style has set a trend. Just as visually unique is the RIBA award-winning Vista house, built by architect Simon Conder: here, the bones of a 1930s wooden fishing hut have been shrink-wrapped in matt black rubber. In contrast, the silver curves of a vintage Airstream caravan parked outside reflect the pale light above. Nearby, other buildings have been improvised out of old railway coaches.

The wonderfully twisted result looks something akin to a frontier community; a far cry from the neatly turned out bungalows of nearby Lydd. Dungeness, even in this already unconventional outpost of Kent, is a defiantly alien place, and one that seems proud to be flouting the normal rules of the British seaside.

OTHER BEACHES

St Mary's Bay is beachier than Dungeness. Long and flat, the pale sand here seems endless when the tide is out. It is not far to the north, between Littlestone-on-Sea and Dymchurch, and the Romney, Hythe and Dymchurch Light Railway stops here. Military historians should look out for the Martello towers, defensive forts built in the 19th century to resist Napoleon. Closer to Dungeness is Romney Sands, another sandy beach with a military flavour; nearby are the concrete 'listening ears'. These aeroplane-detecting sound mirrors were constructed for World War II, but their usefulness was eclipsed by the arrival of radar. *See also pp104-111.*

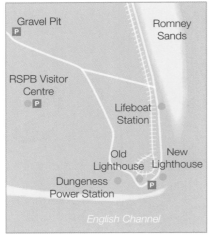

HOW TO GET THERE

By car From Ashford and the M20 take the A2070 towards Brenzett and then the A259 towards New Romney. Turn right on the B2075 towards Lydd. Dungeness is signposted from Lydd. **By train** Take the train to Folkestone and then get a taxi five miles to Hythe to catch the Romney, Hythe and Dymchurch Light Railway. This goes to Dungeness in 65 minutes, timetables vary seasonally (01797 362353, www.rhdr.org.uk). **By bus** Take the 12 to Lydd-on-Sea then two-mile taxi ride (0845 600 2299, www.stagecoachbus.com). Alternatively, take the 11, 11A, 11B bus to Lydd-on-Sea, followed by a two-mile taxi ride

(Kent Coach Tours 01233 627330). Traveline bus (0871 200 2233).

PARKING

Free parking at the Light Railway Café, a five-minute walk from the beach, and at Hythe and New Romney stations.

FACILITIES

Café. Toilets (disabled, nappy-changing facilities) at the Railway. No facilities at Dungeness Point.

SPORTS

Angling. Fishing (Seagull Tackle Shop, Greatstone, 01797 366837).

SWIMMING

Strong currents and undertow – no swimming. Water quality: not MCS tested.

RULES

No barbecues, camping or fires. Dogs are permitted on Dungeness Point (not the RSPB nature reserve).

FURTHER REFERENCE

Folkestone Tourist Information (01303 258594, www.discoverfolkestone. co.uk). RSPB (01797 320588, www.rspb.org.uk). Local council (01303 850388, www.shepway.gov.uk).

Prospect Cottage, once home to Derek Jarman, is Dungeness in a nutshell: strangely beautiful.

WHERE TO STAY AND EAT

Romney Bay House Hotel (0870 418 8063) has a glamorous past. Designed and built in the 1920s for the doyenne of gossip columnists, Hedda Hopper, it is the creation of Sir Clough Williams-Ellis, who also built Portmeirion, the Welsh village made famous by *The Prisoner*. Today, this comfortable ten-bedroom house is noted for its sea views and quietly classy restaurant. Expect modern Anglo-French food prepared with fresh, local ingredients and matched by an excellent wine list. The cream teas are also popular.

White Horses Cottage (01797 366626, www.white-horses-cottage.co.uk), in nearby Greatstone, is a cheaper option. With its oak beams and leaded windows, it was once part of a Sussex farmhouse but was moved to its current site in 1928. All three of the double rooms enjoy a sea view and share one balcony (great for a large group).

Back in Dungeness, the Pilot (01797 320314, www.thepilot.uk.com) is a popular local restaurant. Some say standards have slipped recently, but the atmosphere is jovial and it still serves decent fish and chips and meat pies. Britannia, on Dungeness Point (01797 321959), is a basic pub serving generous portions of fish and chips. Close by is the Light Railway Café, which serves yet more fish and chips and numerous cups of tea.

Botany Bay

Hidden treasure.

'You can imagine you're anywhere in the world here.' So says Kevin Dunmore, the kiosk man at Botany Bay, a hidden cove on the eastern tip of the Kent coast. 'People say it reminds them of Portugal,' he adds, wistfully gazing out into the grey seas of the Dover Strait.

This is certainly the prettiest of the seven little bays that dot this shoreline. All are characterised by their chalk cliffs – the longest continuous stretch of them in Britain – but Botany Bay wins the postcard prize for its much photographed chalk stacks. It is this signature geological feature, rather than the weather, that brings to mind the Algarve.

Despite being halfway between the resorts of Margate and Ramsgate, Botany Bay is not well known. The approach is through quiet suburban streets, and there is little fanfare when you arrive. There are no waltzers, no donkey rides, no chippies, no amusement arcades, no candyfloss, no doughnut dispensers… This is an old-fashioned beach, where you make your own entertainment. And that's its charm.

That, and the cliffs. They dominate this diminutive strand (it's only 600 feet long) sweeping round the sandy cove and framing the sea. Indeed, with the tide in, the bluffs make Botany Bay feel safe and sheltered. But as the water recedes, the beach opens up and the horizons broaden. Time it right and you can walk along the shore to Broadstairs in an hour, clambering over rocks along the way.

Botany Bay may be well hidden, but it has a cult following. Even on an unseasonably chilly Saturday in July, for instance, the soft sandy beach is colonised by hardy families determined to have A Good Day Out. A series of temporary encampments springs up, demarcated by striped windbreaks (available for hire from the kiosk) and small children frantically digging. Sandwiches and crisps are unpacked, beachmats unfurled, newspapers opened and ball games initiated. Children (who, it seems, never feel the cold) pull on their swimming costumes and head, squealing, into the sea, while parents paddle more tentatively or watch from the windbreaks. In the centre of the beach is the sporty Surf Rescue team – tanned young things in red cagoules.

Botany Bay is a social place, and the kiosk, a small, blue wooden building at the foot of the steps, is the hub. 'The variety of people is great,' says Dunmore, who ran the business for four summers in a row. 'Grandparents, families, dogwalkers, school trips, Jo Brand… no two days are the same.' Some customers linger at the kiosk's café tables scoffing snacks, ice-cream and tea. Dads pitch up to hire bodyboards for their kids, or buy coloured nets for rock pooling.

Indeed, rocks are a distinguishing feature of the landscape here. When the tide goes out, the sea reveals an extensive chalk reef – deemed to be the best in Britain – that makes geologists weak at the knees. Pretty chalk pebbles wash up along the tideline, smoothed into ovals, sometimes with worn holes that make odd little faces. 'Rock Doc' walks are organised by the Thanet Coast Project (www.thanetcoast.org.uk), along with Summer Seashore Safaris, where even amateur rockpoolers can turn up starfish, crabs, piddocks and cuttlefish eggs.

Botany Bay's rocky terrain and cliffs endeared it to smugglers, who plied a lucrative trade in the area during the 18th century. Establishments such as the popular chain pub the Captain Digby Inn (above Joss Bay) revel in this unscrupulous past. The landscape shows signs of it too: hidden around the chalk stacks and headland in Kingsgate Bay, a short walk away, there are smugglers' holes carved into the cliffs. Natural caves, eroded by the waves, were also useful for stashing booty.

This section of the Kent coast boasts the longest continuous stretch of chalk cliffs in Britain.

The smugglers may be gone, but this curious corner of the south-east is still a bit of a law unto itself. Pushing into the sea at the foot of the Thames Estuary, the peninsula likes to think of itself as removed from Kent. Once cut off by the Channel, it maintains its 'Isle of Thanet' moniker despite being attached to the mainland for a century. It boasts of being closer to France than to its county town of Maidstone, though culturally it feels closer to 1978.

The busy shipping traffic prevents the sense of remoteness you find on the west coast, but the sands are still pristine, owing to a particularly fastidious beach cleaner.

'It's always lovely down here,' says Lynn Dunmore, Kevin's wife. 'Even when it's raining. We are right on the edge, the most south-easterly point of England. We say to people, ignore the forecast, just come.' As if to prove her point, a dark cloud skirts the cliffs and then heads off in the direction of Dover.

OTHER BEACHES

Kent may not be synonymous with surfing, but Joss Bay (two bays round from Botany) is the choice of the south-east boarders, on account of its decent groundswell. Surfing is at its best here from September to April (lessons and hire can be arranged via www. jossbay.co.uk). Sheltered by white chalky cliffs, the bay was named after notorious 18th-century smuggler Joss Snelling, a local legend who managed to evade the noose and live till the age of 96, smuggling until the end. For his efforts, he was presented to the future Queen Victoria as 'the famous Broadstairs smuggler'. Overlooking the beach, the North Foreland Lighthouse marks the southern entrance to the Thames.

Best known for binge drinking and Tracey Emin, Margate has evolved into an arty enclave. But there's still old-school seaside fun, such as candy floss, waltzers and donkey rides, plus Margate Caves, a network of caverns once used by smugglers, the curious Shell Grotto (www.shellgrotto.co.uk), covered with 4.6 million shells, and a museum of smuggling.

Minnis Bay is an unpretentious sandy bay, great for rock pooling and popular with families. Sailing, windsurfing and seal trips are offered.

The Viking Coastal Trail, a 27-mile cycle route around the Thanet coastline, covers beaches galore, plus smugglers' haunts, dramatic clifftops, historic churches, nature reserves and Dickens' memorabilia (www.vikingcoastaltrail.co.uk).

WHERE TO STAY AND EAT

Botany Bay is sadly lacking in decent hotels and restaurants. Broadstairs, on the other hand, is full of inspiring choices. Timber-boarded and dating back to the 17th and 18th centuries, the Fishermen's Cottages (01843 601996, www.fishermenscottages. co.uk) ooze history and charm.

The grandest address in Broadstairs, the Royal Albion (01843 868071, www. albionbroad stairs.co.uk) was favoured by Dickens. On bustling Albion Street, it's at the heart of the action, with a garden that backs on to the promenade.

Number 68 (01843 609459, 07800 812229, www.number68.co.uk) has the looks – it's a stylish Edwardian guesthouse with exotically themed rooms and a garden – and the location, being just minutes from the town centre.

Closer to the beach, the clifftop Fayreness Hotel (01843 868641, www.fayreness. co.uk) overlooks Kingsgate Bay. The location is great, and there's golf next door, but the ambience is Holiday Inn bland (it's a chain hotel).

Though the kiosk provides sustenance, Botany Bay is not a foodie favourite. Broadstairs, however, is great. Beaches (01843 600065) is a friendly café serving all-day breakfasts, strong Italian coffee, chunky sandwiches, wholesome soups, speciality wines and beers, and gooey cakes. Takeaways are available.

Osteria Pizzeria Posillipo (01843 601133, www.posillipo.co.uk) is a big and bustling, much-lauded pizzeria. Order an impeccable pizza from the wood-fired oven and eat it on the terrace overlooking Viking Bay. Booking is recommended.

When visiting Kent, it is imperative to drink the ales by Shepherd Neame, the county's biggest brewer. The friendly Neptune's Hall pub (01843 861400) offers a good selection, complemented by seasonal guest ales, bar food and tapas, and a beer garden. The bar and restaurant at the Royal Albion also serves it.

Broadstairs is the kind of beach that demands brightly coloured bucket and spades, and an ice-cream in a cone. Get the former in the tourist shop near the Dickens House Museum (www.dickenshouse.co.uk), and the latter at Chiappini's (01843 865 051). Choose from a range of Italian flavours, or order something fancy in a tall glass with a long spoon.

Now a global brand with outlets in Harrods and Selfridges, Morelli's (01843 860050, www.morellisgelato.com) is the original family-run shop. A wonderfully unreconstructed Italian ice-cream parlour, it has been a favourite since the 1930s and still has a jukebox, pink booths and outrageous sundaes.

HOW TO GET THERE

By car From Broadstairs follow the B2052 (it is called Stone Road, then North Foreland Road). Turn off down Percy Avenue, Kingsgate Avenue or Botany Road and follow them to the end. **By train** Trains run to Broadstairs from London Charing Cross and London Victoria. **By bus** National Express coaches run from London Victoria coach station (www.nationalexpress.com).

PARKING

Free parking on Marine Drive (steps to the beach) and Princess Walk (gentle slope).

FACILITIES

Kiosk (www.thebeachkioskatbotanybay kent.co.uk, Apr-Sept weekends and holidays). Toilets.

SPORTS

Bodyboarding. Surfing (for equipment hire, see www.jossbay.co.uk).

SWIMMING

Lifeguards mid June-Sept. Tidal information: www.portoframsgate.co.uk. Water quality: MCS recommended. Blue Flag. Occasional sewer overflows in extreme weather conditions.

RULES

No dogs 15 May-15 September 10am-6pm. Barbecues and camping with permission from the Foreshore office (01843 577274).

FURTHER REFERENCE

Ramsgate Tourist Office (01843 583333, visitthanet.co.uk). Local council (01843 577000, www.thanet.gov.uk). Websites: www.broadstairsfolkweek.org.uk; www.forces-of-nature.co.uk; www. itta-kent.com; www.thanetcoast. org.uk; www.portoframsgate.co.uk.

Dunwich

Catch it while you can.

'I defy anyone, at desolate, exquisite Dunwich, to be disappointed in anything,' said Henry James in 1897. A first-time visitor, used to less subtle sandstrips, may find the great novelist's comment bewildering. You could, for example, be disappointed by the beach at first sight – a sparse grey expanse of pebbles, with a view of Sizewell B twin nuclear power stations in the misty distance. Then there's the tiny town itself, comprising about ten lonely buildings.

So what did James mean? The clue lies in the proximity of the words 'desolate' and 'exquisite'. For the central paradox of this one-horse seaside town is that its appeal is based on what it no longer has to offer. For the last 2,000 years Dunwich has been steadily consumed by the sea, its fragile clay and sand cliffs carved away at an average rate of three feet a year. What you see here is pure physical and metaphorical erosion – a fragmented remnant of a municipality that, in the 13th century, was considered the sixth-most important town in England.

Its past glories are laid bare at Dunwich Museum (01728 648796, open Mar-Oct). The Domesday Book indicates that Dunwich paid an annual tax of 68,000 herrings (more than any other Suffolk port); in the 13th century, as a hub of wool and corn shipping, there were 80 trading ships active in the harbour, and up to 18 parish churches. Dunwich had its own mint and was represented by two members of parliament.

Then came the fateful storm of 14 January 1286: tonnes of upset shingle blocked the entrance to Dunwich harbour, and the town's port became virtually inaccessible to trade. A further, equally vicious storm in 1328 finished off the harbour, while a third, in 1347, claimed 400 houses. With their economy quite literally sunk, and their residences under severe threat, the town's population dissolved faster than the coastline. Soon the remaining tidal defences became untenable.

Of Dunwich's important religious buildings, St Michael's and St Bartholemew's fell to the sea in the early 14th century; St Leonard's and St Martin's succumbed to the waters shortly thereafter. Apart from a fragment of buttress salvaged from All Saints, which toppled in the 17th century, the nearest you can get to them now is by walking through the ruins of Greyfriars monastery, itself perilously close to a watery grave, and looking wistfully out to sea.

Dunwich folklore runs in mythical tandem to the truth. On certain nights, the fisherman's tale goes, you can hear the distant toll of bells rising from the sea. Sitting on the lonely beach with this in mind, you can easily imagine that the white sails of distant boats are ghostly church spires rising from the waves. Certainly the town's history of loss, or indeed the sight of octogenarian coach parties arriving at the Flora Tea Rooms, backs up the sense of gloom; not to mention the fact that, until recently, bones from the old All Saints cemetery could be seen protruding from the cliffs.

When Turner and Constable each committed the beach to canvas, they captured a gloriously ghostly landmark, one where each footfall contributes to further decay. There are few places in Britain that showcase the ravages of time – and water – like Dunwich, which, at one time, was connected to the Netherlands. Here, the sea is no gentle mantle: it is a catalyst and agent of destruction, 'a ruminating beast', to quote James again, 'an insatiable, indefatigable lip'.

So it is a sweet irony that Dunwich, a district for so many years known for its depopulation and geographical dereliction, is also the site of so much life and regeneration. That desolate, exquisite beach backs on to a teeming heath, two of the

largest reedbeds in Britain, and a woodland where red stags can be heard rutting in autumn. The gentle roads in between cry out for cyclists, and there are plenty of places to stop off for a picnic; a walk along the beach, though, will give you more to think about.

The glittering shingle is not the easiest of walking surfaces, and it's a case of two steps forward, one step back for much of the trek. Nevertheless, it's a stimulating hour's journey from Dunwich car park to the birdlands. On the way, you'll pass children throwing stones into the water, the braver ones taking the plunge themselves. The odd fisherman can be found dug into the pebbles at the water's edge, with his wife sitting dutifully behind him. Dunwich is renowned for bass, which scavenge in the surf in summer, while cod rise to the bait in winter.

Dunwich Heath, run by the National Trust, is a major draw to the new generation of fans. Committed walkers and more tentative wilderness explorers can both benefit from a ramble through this beautiful patch, which glows with bright purple heather in the summer. Butterflies, bees and dragonflies patrol the air, while adders, slow worms and grass snakes can occasionally be spotted retreating from the paths, slithering away in deference to heavy-footed walkers.

Dunwich may lack sand and surf culture, but it is renowned for bass and cod fishing.

Birdwatchers are in their element here, but the best sightings are at nearby Minsmere, about ten minutes' drive from the beach. Here, the RSPB protects a vast number of bird species. The Dartford warbler returned to breed in Suffolk in the 1990s after a 50-year absence from the country. Similarly, the avocet was extinct in Britain until 1947, when it returned to Minsmere (the RSPB features the bird on its logo). Two marsh harriers

spotted nesting at the sanctuary in 1971 became the Adam and Eve of the 350 pairs counted in Britain in 2005. The reserve also holds more than a quarter of the UK bittern population. It is this reserve that holds the hope for the future of Dunwich: a lifeline for British birds, it has incubated a tourism revival that will keep Dunwich on the map – until it literally disappears off the map.

Finally, for the really brave, Dunwich has become the finishing point for a challenging excursion. The Dunwich Dynamo (www.southwarkcyclists.org.uk) is an annual overnight cycle leaving Hackney in London on the Saturday in July that falls nearest the full moon. About 500 people participate annually in the 120-mile ride. Why Dunwich? 'It's partly about the attraction of this big road to nowhere,' says Patrick Field of the London School of Cycling. 'Also, the journey gets shorter every year.'

OTHER BEACHES

Though it lacks the historical-poetic appeal of Dunwich, nearish neighbour Aldeburgh is a more action-packed place to visit. The shingle beach – like Dunwich, a cause for geographical concern – attracts more visitors. Second-home owners have bought up a good deal of real estate, bringing with them organic food shops, swanky cafés and boutiquey shops. The annual Aldeburgh Festival (www.aldeburgh.co.uk, 01728 687110) was developed by the town's most famous former resident, Benjamin Britten. Britten is buried at the church of St Peter and St Paul's, and he is commemorated by Maggi Hambling's sculpture *The Scallop*, a mammoth stainless steel shell structure which divided the critics when it was unveiled in 2003. Adding to the haunting atmosphere, it is

engraved with the words 'I hear those voices that will not be drowned' from Britten's opera *Peter Grimes*. The Aldeburgh Museum (01728 454666, www.aldeburghmuseum.org.uk) gives interesting background to this former Victorian seaside resort.

WHERE TO STAY AND EAT

Cliff House Holiday Park (01728 658282, www.cliffhouseholidays.co.uk) is a 30-acre holiday site that offers the works: tent and caravan plots, static caravans, apartments, cottages and log cabins. It has direct access to the beach, and is adjacent to both Dunwich Heath and the RSPB sanctuary at Minsmere. Dunwich town is about five minutes' drive.

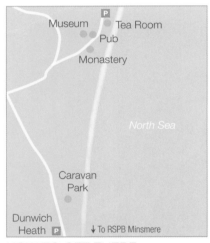

Map

Museum
Tea Room P
Pub
Monastery
North Sea
Caravan Park
Dunwich Heath P
↓ To RSPB Minsmere

HOW TO GET THERE

By car From Bury-St-Edmunds, take the A143 north to Bungay, then the A144 south. At the A12 turn left towards Lowestoft; the B1387 (Walberswick) and the B1125 (Leiston) will take you as far as signs for Dunwich. **By train** Nearest rail station is Darsham, then Coastlink bus to Dunwich. **By bus** Contact Traveline, or Suffolk County Council, for up-to-date information (0871 200 2233, www.traveline.co.uk). Coastlink (01728 833526), a minibus service, will meet you at train stations if you book in advance, and take you to Dunwich.

PARKING

Free parking at the beach. At Dunwich Heath £4 (free for NT members).

FACILITIES

Café. Toilets (disabled).

SPORTS

Angling (01728 453088, or Angling Southwold Angling Centre, 01502 722085). Sailing (Aldeburgh Yacht Club, 01728 452562, www.aldeburghyc. u-net.com).

SWIMMING

Permitted (no lifeguard or emergency facilities). Water quality: not MCS tested.

RULES

No barbecues or camping. No climbing on the cliffs. Dogs permitted.

FURTHER REFERENCE

Aldeburgh Tourist Information Centre (01728 453637, www.suffolkcoastal. gov.uk/tourism). RSPB Minsmere (01728 648281, www.rspb.org.uk). Local council (01473 583000, www.suffolkcc.gov.uk). Websites: www.suffolkcoastal.gov.uk; www.nationaltrust.org.uk.

The ghostly ruins of Greyfriars Monastery are perched precariously close to the sea.

For fans of film trivia, Cliff House itself was once owned by Jock Horsfall, an Aston Martin driver who was involved in Operation Mincemeat in World War II, which formed the basis for the film *The Man Who Never Was*.

The Thorpeness Hotel (01728 452176, www.thorpeness.co.uk), in nearby Aldeburgh, might make for a more comfortable stay than the Dunwich-based Ship Inn (01728 648219, www.shipinndunwich.co.uk), the nearest pub to the beach itself. Though simply decorated, it is nevertheless a charming place to relax, and serves good fish and chips.

But the best fish and chips in Dunwich are found at the Flora Tea Rooms (01728 648433). Brill and skate are specialities, in addition to cod and haddock. It also serves home-made cakes and ice-cream sundaes. Check out the irresistibly naff tea-towels.

Away from the beach, the National Trust-run Coastguard Cottage Tea Rooms (01728 648501) overlook the heath. Quiches, soups and filled rolls make up the bulk of the food, but don't miss the delicious own-made cakes.

Southwold

A very English experience.

This section of the Suffolk coast was declared an Area of Outstanding Natural Beauty back in 1970, and the award is richly deserved. Blots on the landscape are few and far between, but even the imposing white dome of Sizewell B nuclear power station, clearly visible on all but the mistiest of days, is surprisingly inoffensive to the eye. Southwold's Blue Flag beach is as civilised as the town that backs it, with golden sands, spanking new groynes and a vast line of well-maintained beach huts. These form a handsome backdrop, sporting cheery names such as Bonaventure and Happy Days, along with price tags that would buy a family house in less desirable parts of East Anglia. This is middle-class, Middle England par excellence, and families spread out of their little huts on to the promenade replete with all the requirements of a perfect beach day in Blighty: deckchairs, sandwiches, teapot and copies of the Sunday papers. This is one patch of English coastline joyfully devoid of unnatural distractions – as local celebrity PD James once wrote: 'In Southwold one feels that escapism is a positive virtue.'

On a hot, sunny June day, it's hard to imagine a more civilised spot in the land, but come back in January and civility soon gives way to severe weather as the Arctic winds roll in. By then, the beach huts have long since departed on a forklift truck for the safety of the car park, where they sit in colourful hibernation until the return of spring. To combat the ravages of the wintry North Sea, there is a sharp drop from the promenade to the beach below, with stone steps every hundred yards or so. To avoid any unnecessary inconvenience, beach hut regulars set up their own ladders to access the sand, and like a scene from a Heath Robinson sketch, spend their days scuttling from toe-dipping to tea-drinking and vice versa.

The pier, meanwhile, is in keeping with the town: simple, tasteful and classy, largely devoid of Brightonesque honky-tonk or razzle-dazzle (though it has one tiny arcade with a few mad, arty slot machines). And, like the town, the pier is enjoying a renaissance, after a 2001 revamp returned it to sparkling form.

Further along the beach towards Walberswick, the beach huts finally fade out to give way to a less ordered stretch of sand, backed by dunes rather than 'Dun Roamins'. This southern strand, known locally as the Denes, is eventually blocked by the estuary of the River Blyth, the divide between calm river and churned-up sea clearly visible between the harbour walls. Centuries of storms have driven Southwold's port further and further inland, and now the few remaining fishing boats from the town's once impressive fleet nestle quietly a few hundred yards up the estuary away from the sea, flanked by the wooden huts from where they sell their catch. There is no sand here, but in its place are rows of locals and holidaymakers indulging in a spot of crabbing, armed only with a line, a bucket and a hunk of the crustaceans' favourite tipple, bacon. The blue riband event is the British Open Crabbing Championship, held every August on the banks of the river. The basic idea is simple: over a 90-minute period, and armed only with a single line and bait of your choice, the person landing the single heaviest crab wins. A fee of £1 is payable to enter, and all equipment (buckets, bait and line) is available on site for a small charge.

Southwold is an appealing slice of seaside nostalgia, from the lovely pier and stately architecture to the low-key crowd.

Last year, Oscar Kane walked away with first prize, beating off more than 700 competitors with a crab weighing 5.75oz. If none of the little nippers bite, then the Sole Bay Fish Company dispenses divine dressed crab from its converted fishing huts. With just ten yards from river to plate, it doesn't get much fresher than this.

Crosswords and crustaceans are all very well, but what really sells Southwold as a beach destination, apart from the fact that its golden sands beat the shingle of Aldeburgh hands down, is the very town itself, which is as cultured as coastal resorts come, from Jill Freud's summer theatre season and November's Ways with Words literature festival to the 19th-century lighthouse and handsome Georgian high street, filled with all manner of life from posh delis to Denny, a department store that has tailored everyone from George Orwell to Benjamin Britten over the years. The invasion of the SHOs (second-home owners) may have proved a mixed blessing with oppressive summer traffic, both human and motorised, and locals being priced out of the property market, but there is still a strong sense of spirit about the place.

A lot of that spirit is down to the town's biggest employer and supplier of the wonderful aroma of malt that lingers around the town – Adnams brewery. And if you need to clear your head after a few too many pints of its fine Broadside the night before, then there's no better hangover cure than a bracing stroll along the promenade, with the waves of the North Sea crashing below.

OTHER BEACHES

Walberswick is a 15-mile drive from Southwold, but it is a mere five-minutes by charming ferryboat across the River Blyth from Southwold Harbour. The village was a regular retreat of Charles Rennie Mackintosh and Philip Wilson Steer, whose Impressionist views of the beach can be seen at the Tate Britain, and its chocolate-box cottages still hide a selection of artistic stowaways and media luvvies entranced by this corner of the Sunrise Coast. The village is no undiscovered gem, and the huge car park down by the river soon fills up on a sunny Sunday, but the day-tripping crowds do nothing to blight the charm of the place. The beach, a few minutes' walk across the dunes from the handsome village green, is a beautiful expanse of sand, with a more rugged feel than Southwold's ordered prom, and backed by coastal grass and little else. Walberswick's charms stretch inland as well; the nature reserve that follows the tidal estuary of the River Blyth is a haven of peace away from the beach. Made up of heathland, reedbeds, mudflats, grazing marsh, hay meadows and woodland, the reserve is home to otter and deer, plus more than 240 species of bird. Dunwich and Aldeburgh (pp128-135) are just south of here.

WHERE TO STAY AND EAT

Acton Lodge (01502 723217, www.southwold.ws/actonlodge) is a handsome villa by South Green with views towards Walberswick and Dunwich. Original features (marble fireplaces, stripped floors) have been preserved; bedrooms are spacious.

The Crown Hotel (01502 722275, www.adnams.co.uk/hotels) is pub, wine bar, restaurant and small hotel in one. It started life as a humble posting inn called the Nag's

Head. Now owned and restored in pastel hues by Adnams, it's a smaller, cheaper and less classy sibling to the Swan (*see below*). There are 14 simply decorated but fully equipped rooms, some with exposed beams. Food is a strong point, but the no-reservations policy is frustrating. Fortunately, the gastro fare is almost worth the wait.

The self-assured Swan (01502 722186, www.adnams.co.uk/hotels) has long been the hub of Southwold social life. There are 26 bedrooms in the main hotel and a further 17 garden rooms. The handsome dining room overlooks Southwold's market place and the food is a cut above. A class act.

The best pubs in Southwold are those that allow alfresco spillover during fine weather, and the best of the bunch is the wonderfully atmospheric Lord Nelson (01502 722079), between Market Hill and the sea. In summer, you can take your pint of Adnams to the seafront or sit in the walled patio out the back. In winter, the fire is lit and the atmosphere is cosy, verging on crowded.

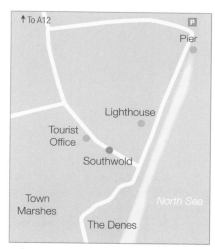

HOW TO GET THERE

By car Take the A12 to Blythburgh; just after the village, turn right on to the A1095 to Southwold. **By train** The nearest stations are Darsham or Halesworth, which are about ten miles away. **By bus** Local bus services are provided by Anglian Coaches (01502 711109, www.anglianbus.co.uk).

PARKING

Pay and display car park next to the pier. Free on-street parking in town.

FACILITIES

Beach hut hire (from £110/wk; 01502 723292). Campsite (01502 722486). Toilets (disabled, nappy-changing).

SPORTS

Fishing (www.beachfishing.org.uk). Kayaking (Southwold Canoe Group, 01502 478532). Sailing (www.southwold sailing.co.uk). Surfing. Windsurfing.

SWIMMING

There is a lifeguard by the pier late May-early Sept, but not by the Denes. Water quality: MCS recommended, Blue Flag by pier. The Denes: MCS recommended, Quality Coast Award.

RULES

No barbecues or camping. Dogs permitted on leads 1 Oct-30 Apr.

FURTHER REFERENCE

Southwold Tourist Information Centre (01502 724729, www.visit-southwold. co.uk). Local council (01502 562111, www.waveney.gov.uk). Website: www.exploresouthwold.co.uk.

Holkham

Wide open spaces.

For views encompassing huge swathes of sky, sand and sea, look no further than Holkham. If you saw *Shakespeare in Love*, you'll already know how beautiful this Norfolk beach is – it featured in the closing sequence of that film. It's a knockout even on the dullest and dampest of days, when the palette of colours runs from dove grey to slate and the beach is perfect for long contemplative walks. The only occasion that doesn't offer magnificent views is when the fog rolls in, and then the place acquires an eerie desolation magnified by the sound of unseen birds passing overhead. But in sunshine, the beach is astonishing, with views in every direction and something of interest whichever way you look – even behind you.

Holkham is backed by a majestic stretch of pine woods and dunes. Not only a stunning backdrop, the forest provides walkers with shelter from winter gales and children with tree-climbing, rope-swinging and hide-and-seek opportunities, not to mention a scenic approach to the beach: the journey from the car park is along a boardwalk through the woodland. The car park is no eyesore, either: surrounded by flat fields and marshland, it is often full of migrating birds.

True, on a sunny bank holiday weekend, the car park can get packed, but there's always plenty of room on the beach, thanks to its vast size and the dearth of public transport. At low tide, the sand seems to stretch forever, making it easy to get away from the crowds – it just depends how far you're prepared to walk.

Take a moment to survey the scene from the raised viewing point at the end of the boardwalk. Down on the beach, there's a huge patch of salt marsh to be negotiated; after that, it's sand, rock pools and dunes as far as the eye can see. On warm days, sandcastles, swimming and beach games take priority; on windswept days, walking, horseriding and kite-flying come to the fore (even in summer, clued-up regulars bring a windbreak with them, as the sands are pretty exposed on this part of the Norfolk coast).

Turn left at the end of the boardwalk and after about 20 minutes you get to the part of the beach used by naturists; turn right and after about two miles you arrive at Wells-next-the-Sea, identified by a jaunty row of beach huts.

The colourful cluster comes as a surprise after the bare expanses of Holkham, which happily has no facilities of any kind – no shop, no snack bar, no loos (the one concession is an upmarket snack truck in the car park, serving the likes of venison sandwiches, soup and ice-cream, in season). It's kept unspoiled by the Holkham Estate, which owns the land for miles around. Its showpiece is Holkham Hall (01328 710227, www.holkham.co.uk), a Palladian extravaganza. Across the main road from the beach, the stately home is open on selected days in summer; the grounds stay open for a longer period.

The beach may lack amenities, but it has an abundance of wildlife. Holkham is packed with interest for naturalists: sea lavender covers the salt marsh in the summer, and the dunes host a variety of flowers and grasses. The sand dunes are also popular with nesting birds – when necessary, sections of the beach are cordoned off to give colonies of little terns some space and a chance to rear their offspring. And birds are a huge attraction here: Titchwell Marsh Nature Reserve (01485 210779, www.rspb.org.uk), a wetland reserve run by the Royal Society for the Protection of Birds, is just along the coast. You'll see plenty of twitchers on and around Holkham beach, and no wonder. As well as many varieties of ducks and geese, the landscape draws sandmartins, redshanks, marsh harriers and curlew sandpipers.

Twitchers take second place to walkers, however. Holkham is on the Norfolk Coastal Path, an ancient route that can be followed west for a two-mile hike along the salt marshes.

Not a bad range of activities and sights for a beach that, at first glance, looks like an empty – albeit stunning – expanse.

OTHER BEACHES

The woodland provides shelter for walkers, and fun and games for children.

If you want a beach with bells and whistles, head two miles east of Holkham to the little town of Wells-next-the-Sea, which manages to cram in a beach resort, fishing port, picturesque shopping street and light railway. It's also the nearest point for good fish and

Norfolk

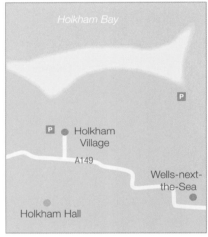

HOW TO GET THERE

By car Turn off the A149 down Lady Anne's Drive (opposite the Victoria hotel) at Holkham village. **By train** The nearest station is King's Lynn, then 30 miles by taxi or bus. **By bus** Coasthopper bus 36 (01553 776980, www.norfolkgreen.co.uk).

PARKING

Pay parking £3/day.

FACILITIES

Holkham: Snack trailer during high season. Wells: Café/restaurant. Campsite. First aid post. Slipway. Shop. Toilets (disabled).

SPORTS

Cycling (Norfolk Coast Cycleway, accessed from Wells; map, £2 available from Wells TIC). Fishing trips (01485 512474, www.norfolkfishingtrips.co.uk). Horse riding on beach (only with permit from Holkham Estate, 01328 710227). Windsurfing (with permit, 01328 711646).

SWIMMING

Care must be taken due to strong tidal currents. Swim between red and yellow flags. Lifeguard weekends mid Mar to end Oct; no emergency facilities. Coastguard (Wells-next-the-Sea, 01328 710219). Water quality: MCS basic pass.

RULES

No barbecues, camping or fires. No dogs permitted on certain parts of the beach all year round; see signs. Litter and dog waste bins provided.

FURTHER REFERENCE

Wells Tourist Information Centre, Wells-next-the-Sea (01328 710885, www.visit northnorfolk.com). Local council (01553 616200, www.west-norfolk.gov.uk). Websites: www.countryfairoffice.co.uk; www.norfolkcoastaonb.org.uk; www. wells-next-the-sea.net.

chips. Further along are the seaside villages of Blakeney (home to a three-mile sand and shingle spit) and Cley-next-the-Sea (more pebbles). Boat trips to view the seals at Blakeney Point are run from the quay at Morston and also from Cley. Go west along the A149 and you arrive at Brancaster Staithe (a glorious stretch of sand), Titchwell Marsh Nature Reserve and Holme-next-the-Sea (a slightly hidden – and therefore delightfully quiet – sandy beach), and finally at the seaside resort of Hunstanton. In between these beaches are small roads leading to creeks and marshes – all worth exploring if you have the time, and don't crave a bucket and spade experience.

WHERE TO STAY AND EAT

The Holkham Estate runs the opulently decorated Victoria Hotel (01328 711008, www. victoriaatholkham.co.uk), at the gates of Holkham Hall. The only place to stay within walking distance of the beach, it isn't cheap, but it has an easy-going charm. Popular with both romantic breakers and families, it's often fully booked. The restaurant and bar are open to non-residents, but book in advance, except on the most desolate of winter days.

Just a few yards along the main road is the handsome Marsh Larder Tearooms, also estate-run, which does a great line in cakes and savouries.

One village to the east, in Wells-next-the-Sea, is the Globe Inn (01328 710206, www.globeatwells.co.uk), which offers rooms, local ales from Adnams and Woodfordes and decent food. Wells also has Pinewoods holiday park (01328 710439, www.pinewoods.co.uk), which hosts a mix of caravans, tents and beach huts.

A short drive along the coast in the other direction, the Lifeboat Inn (Ship Lane, Thornham, 01485 512236, www.lifeboatinn.co.uk) is a pleasantly ramshackle old pub with rooms. It serves a crowd-pleasing bar menu (bowls of mussels, fish and chips), alongside real ales, in a relaxed atmosphere: dogs, children, muddy boots – all are welcome.

Smarter, but still welcoming, are local hotels the George (01263 740652, www. thegeorgehotelcley.com) in Cley-next-the-Sea and the Hoste Arms (01328 738777, www.hostearms.co.uk) in Burnham Market; both have restaurants.

Stretching as far as the eye can see and often empty, the beach at Holkham is made for walking.

Runswick Bay

A northern star.

You won't see Runswick Bay until the last second – but what a first impression it makes. After navigating a winding road through farmland and a bland suburban pocket, you come across a small wooden sign, pointing quietly to the beach. Suddenly, at the crest of a hill, a glorious panorama opens up. As you launch down the precipitous dead-end road, the bay spreads out beneath you. Pause and take it in from on high. On a fine day its beauty is uncomplicated; on a grey or foggy day it has a mystic grip. In the foreground, a gently curving arc of sand, nearly a mile long, is backed by hills covered, almost tropically, by impenetrable bushes and trees. Beyond, the foreshore turns rocky and cliffs rise steeply to the dramatic headland of Kettleness.

Not until you reach the bottom of the hill does the village of Runswick Bay reveal itself to the west. It is absurdly pretty – Yorkshire gone soft. Some 90 cottages, all built of honey-coloured stone and gaily topped with red pantiles, are packed in against the cliff. Stone-flagged footpaths wind in and out of cottages with names like Bay View, Capstan, Fisherman and Cockpit House. Gardens with picket fences spill with roses, hollyhocks, delphiniums, valerian and geraniums, even a Riviera palm – all framed at every turn by the comforting arm of the bay.

No wonder the Victorians painted it. In particular, the Staithes Group colony of 'plein air' painters were irresistibly drawn to the scene. They were led by Dame Laura Knight and her husband Harold Knight, who settled three miles north, and the pioneering Whitby photographer Frank Meadow Sutcliffe. And at the centre of their pictures, at the water's edge, is invariably the cutest property of all: Lady Palmer's Cottage, thatched and whitewashed. Once the coastguard house, now part of the Marquis of Normanby's dominant local estate, it has remained otherwise unchanged for a century.

Nothing much changes in Runswick. Nothing unsightly disturbs the postcard. No roads, no cars, no shops – save a café selling paper flags to top off sandcastles – no restaurants, no amusements, no donkeys, no deckchairs. Simple joys come from sandcastles and picnics, beach cricket and rock pooling, fossil hunting and cliff-top walks. A cormorant dries its wings on an exposed rock; a brave surfer rides a North Sea wave at Cobble Dump; both are sleek and black.

The fishermen have long gone. The only ones remaining are hobby fishermen with a line or two for mackerel, whiting and ling, and a handful of licensed lobster fishermen in summer. Once, a fleet of 20 cobles (the flat-bottomed fishing boats unique to these parts) sailed out of Runswick, their long lines baited with limpets collected from the shore by the 'flither girls'.

It was an insular community, where the excise man had little chance of catching smugglers and where tragedy at sea was a given. In 1664, for instance, a landslip caused the whole village to fall into the sea; casualties were low, but only one house survived.

When fishing declined after World War I, Runswick turned to modest tourism. A pretty wooden café, now the sailing club, was erected at the end of the beach. Fishermen ran boat trips round the bay and rented out changing tents on the beach for the wealthy mill-owners, who arrived by train from the smoky West Riding towns.

A handful of green wooden huts, set back on the bank, are the last of their original holiday homes. With no electricity or running water, they conjure images of simple summer holidays – barbecues, beachcombing – but the Marquis's estate won't allow them to be sold or let. Instead, the fishermen's cottages command the highest prices on the Yorkshire coast. And yet the permanent population has dwindled to less than 20; on a winter's day the village is soulless, like an abandoned film set.

Still, many of the cottages are available to let in summer. Children play on the beach, swim and bodyboard safely, and scamper – cold, wet and salty – to the Sandside Café,

Rocky cliffs, dramatic headlands and rich greenery characterise the scenery at Runswick Bay.

where the Cole family have been serving tea and cakes, ices and fizzy floats since the 1950s. For something stronger, the Royal pub has a small terrace facing the sea and is a welcome stop for walkers following the Cleveland Way, the coast path that runs along much of the cliff top. In the back bar, a stash of games comes in handy on rainy days. On the wall, there are old photographs of the Runswick Rescue Boat, financed and run by the villagers – a tradition dating back to 1866. The occasional windsurfer or dinghy sailor in trouble is extremely glad of it.

In winter, the pub's opening hours are much reduced, like everything else in these parts. But winter is the best time of year for fossiling: the friable cliffs of Lower Jurassic rock and shale disgorge fossils dating back 180 million years. Sharp-eyed visitors can find ammonites, belemnites or jet – the fossilised monkey puzzle tree that is still made into jewellery. As recently as 1999, the cliff disgorged an ichthyosaur, though it was no match for the plesiosaur found here in 1848. At 22 feet long and 13 feet across, the latter was the largest complete reptile ever discovered along the Yorkshire coast.

Beach cricket, beachcombing and seal spotting: three of Runswick Bay's simple pleasures.

Such magnificent finds were unearthed by the wholesale quarrying of the Kettleness end of the bay in the 19th century. Alum, a mineral found in the shale deposits, was essential as a fixative for dyes. But the complex process required urine, and local residents were paid a penny a bucket to supply it.

To reach Kettleness, pass the bright blue wooden sailing club and chase the turnstones and oystercatchers along the water's edge. Soon a narrow cleft appears in the cliff and you will rejoin the Cleveland Way with a stiff climb. At the top, there is a disused railway, but most people follow the path. From this lofty vantage point, you may see a pair of high-speed peregrine falcons quartering, or a seal or porpoise below.

The hamlet of Kettleness marks the end of the bay. There was once a Roman signalling station in the fields here, but there are no facilities today except for a pair of wooden benches from which you can survey the weird lunar landscape of the alum workings, and then pan back slowly over the sands to the village. The view is guaranteed to take the breath away.

OTHER BEACHES

South of Runswick, lovely little Sandsend is a seaside village with a 1950s vibe. Its wide, clean beach stretches all the way to Whitby. And the estuary is safe and shallow, a good place for small children to play, paddle and sail their inflatable dinghies.

Whitby, further south still, is Runswick's most famous neighbour. At West Cliff, take the zigzag path down to a wonderful two-mile stretch of sand. Here are deckchairs and windbreaks, ice-creams and beach huts – on a sunny afternoon, you can do no better. If the steep climb back is too daunting, take the cliff lift up to the top (in summer only).

North of Runswick, Staithes is a quaint old-fashioned village with a pocket handkerchief-sized beach, but there is plenty of simple fun to be had by sailing dinghies across the harbour to the lifeboat station. At low tide, there is a stunning stretch of rock or scar on which to walk and rockpool.

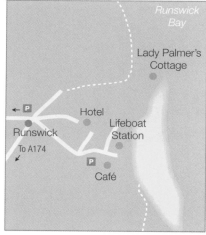

HOW TO GET THERE

By car From Whitby, take the A174 north for five miles, turn right at Ellerby at the sign for Runswick Bay. Continue for one mile until you reach the top of the village; turn right down steep hill. From the north, take the A174. Turn left at the end of Hinderwell village by the war memorial. Continue for one mile until you reach the top of village. Turn right down steep hill.

PARKING

Pay and display car park in the lower village. In summer, there is parking in the top car park opposite the Cliffemount Hotel.

FACILITIES

Toilets (in the lower village).

SPORTS

Sailing. Waterskiing (both at Runswick Bay Beach and Sailing Club, www.rbbsc.co.uk).

SWIMMING

Shallow shelf, no undertow. No lifeguard. No access to beach at highest tide. Tide tables available at the Royal pub. Runswick Bay Rescue Boat (www. runswickrescue.co.uk). Staithes and Runswick Lifeboat: dial 999 and ask for coastguard. Water quality: MCS recommended. Quality Coast Award.

RULES

Dogs permitted.

FURTHER REFERENCE

Whitby Tourist Information Centre (01947 602674, www.visitwhitby. com). Local council (01723 232323, www.scarborough.gov.uk).

WHERE TO STAY AND EAT

A cosy mix of stone cottages and winding paths, the village has long been a magnet for artists.

Pretty self-catering cottages are the classic Runswick Bay accommodation. Some owners add their names to a list available from the Royal pub; others are let through an agency. The Ingrid Flute Agency in Scarborough (01723 376777, www.ingridflute.co.uk) has a good selection. A couple with good sea views are Marlin Spike and Ebor House.

Cockpit House (01947 840504) is Runswick Bay's only B&B and is comfortable and homely, with great breakfasts. There is a clean but basic caravan and camping site at the top of the village (Runswick Bay Camping and Caravan Park, 01947 840997).

In Staithes, the next village along, the Endeavour Restaurant with Rooms (01947 840825, www.endeavour-restaurant.co.uk) has four comfortable en suite bedrooms with the bonus of a really good seafood restaurant.

An excellent sea view is what distinguishes the Royal pub (01947 602234). The terrace is a fine place to enjoy sandwiches, chips and a pint of Black Sheep. In winter, it is open only for lunch from Monday to Thursday, and often closes around Christmas.

Sandside Café (01947 840224) has great views and provides good but simple sandwiches, scones and cakes. For something more substantial, the tiny hamlet of Goldsborough has the wonderful Fox and Hounds (01947 893372), which has a short but excellent menu served in the lounge or garden.

Bamburgh

Castles in the sand.

The dunes run on for miles and the castle looms large. Offshore you can see the Farne Islands shimmering in the distance. It's an extraordinary scene, but yet it is ordinary too. A father is making slovenly, old-fashioned footballer moves and running rings round his bored nine-year-old; a young couple are taking the sun behind a windbreak; many people are simply walking and talking. That's Bamburgh in a nutshell: a spectacular backdrop for a low-key day at the beach.

Just behind the beach, in Bamburgh village, there is an immaculate green, a quaint row of early 19th-century buildings converted to tea rooms and shops, and a backside perspective of that grand castle, so stylistically perfect you almost expect Crusaders in red-crossed tunics to come storming out on war horses at any moment. The entire locale is so suggestive of an idealised sense of Englishness – albeit the northern version – that it takes an enormous feat of will to conceive of it as anything else. Then again…

Romans came in the first century AD, ruled over the local Celtic tribes, then left by the early fifth century. Soon thereafter the Angles turned up, Germano-Danish invaders from the inscrutable east. Eventually, the Angles, and their Saxon cousins, took over the entire country. Later Viking sallies were seen off, but not the Norman conquest of the 11th century, of course. Out of this tumbling disequilibrium came the basis for England: a Norman aristocracy taxing an emulsion of Anglo-Saxons and Romano-Celts.

But in the blink of an historical eye, back during the fifth and sixth centuries, a coastal stronghold sited here called Din Guardi was the centre of a British kingdom known as Bryneich – latterly Bernicia – the land of mountain passes. This was the time of Arthur, mistily remembered, or created, by later romantic writers, the last aboriginal resistance to foreign, Angle and Saxon encroachment: heroic and ultimately doomed. This was also the time when the original Bamburgh castle was built, back in 547, by an invading Angle chieftain named Ida the Flamebearer; his fortress was subsequently christened Bebbanburgh, after the wife of a later Anglian monarch, then shortened to Bamburgh.

The current Bamburgh Castle stands on the same spot as that Dark Age redoubt. It was destroyed by Vikings, rebuilt by Normans in the 12th century, held by the monarchs of England, then passed back to private hands. That the castle currently enjoys a rude and structural health is largely thanks to Victorian industrialist and armaments magnate William Armstrong, who bought it in 1894 and returned it to splendour.

Though the castle is Bamburgh's showpiece, the beach is a star in its own right, with remarkably broad appeal. Visitors strolling the sands or puffing up and down the rambling dune system usually have one of three mindsets. First, Bamburgh offers a classic English atmosphere – village green and picnics within earshot of the sea. Then there is the steady trickle of history buffs, soaking up the Celtic and Arthurian spirits from around 1,500 years ago, gazing wistfully at the Farnes and pondering Anglian invaders. But most people simply come for exercise, enjoyment and sea air, not Brookesian visions of England made flesh, or ailing Fisher Kings.

Whatever the motivation, there is more than enough space for all. The beach is sprawling, running from the lighthouse at Harkness Rocks – just north of Bamburgh village – for three miles down to the larger village of Seahouses. At low tide, with a wide

Bamburgh and the spectacular beaches of Northumberland are one of Britain's best-kept secrets.

strand, you can walk the whole way. It is also clean and pristine, as the bracing North Sea winds have blown away any prospect of mass tourism – and with it any prospect of mess, litter and architectural eyesores. Virtually the only building on the beach is the castle, while the Inner Farne Islands, a mile out to sea, are the focal point of the horizon.

The Outer Farnes, three miles offshore, were the site of a celebrated 1838 rescue. One rough autumn night a ship ran aground on Harcar Rocks, so the lighthouse keeper from nearby Longstone Island, William Darling, rowed out to pick up survivors – with help from his 22-year-old daughter Grace. She became an iconic heroine of the period and Bamburgh is home to the Grace Darling Museum, run by the Royal National Lifeboat Institution (www.rnli.org.uk). Back then, they did like their heroines unsullied and tragic, however: Grace died of tuberculosis just short of her 27th birthday, unmarried.

For those who prefer wildlife to Victorian morbidity, Farnes has grey seals and seabirds galore, and there are regular boat trips to the islands from Seahouses in season.

Back on the beach, local species include families, dog walkers, occasional surfers, kite enthusiasts, kids splashing in the breaking waves and other characters – many congregated at the northern end by the village, fewer as you head south.

Backing the entire strand, the dunes are home to assorted birds, rare plants and insects, and were declared a Site of Special Scientific Interest in 1995. The casual visitor might be hard pushed to identify petalwort, or distinguish between two species of

warbler, but the sheer shape, texture and size of those dunes hold allure for the expert and amateur alike. Climb to a high point, marram grass mingling with sand, and you will get an impressive perspective of the dune system, the sweep of the Northumberland coast and the Farnes – but the pre-eminent feature is still that castle: Din Guardi, Bebbanburgh, Bamburgh, beach sentinel. You can't miss it, nor should you.

OTHER BEACHES

It's not a beach in the traditional sense. But the other coastal feature that qualifies as a 'must-see' is Holy Island, just a few miles north of Bamburgh. It has many claims to fame: this is where St Aidan came to found a monastery in the seventh century; it is the birthplace of the Lindisfarne Gospels. And it is highly atmospheric (it still has the ruins of an 11th-century Benedictine priory). The striking 16th-century Holy Island Castle is another highlight. Purchased by Edward Hudson, the founder of *Country Life* magazine, in 1901, it was then transformed into a family home by Edward Lutyens. The island is also a birdwatching hot spot. It is only accessible at low tide, when you can drive or walk across a sand-fringed causeway. For tidal times, check www.northumberlandlife.org/holy-island.

Ross Back Sands are more of a traditional beach spectacular. Between Holy Island and Bamburgh, they are relatively inaccessible, but stunning: with three golden miles, you come here to get away from the crowds (drive in via the minor roads north-east of Belford village, park at the hamlet of Ross, then walk for a mile).

In the opposite direction, there is a strip of beaches south of Seahouses: Beadnell Bay with its harbour and big caravan park; the splendidly named, if tiny, Football Hole; picturesque Embleton Bay with the ruins of Dunstanburgh Castle at the south end; and eventually Alnmouth Bay and Druridge Bay, the latter closest of all to the Newcastle/ Gateshead metropolitan area.

WHERE TO STAY AND EAT

With the castle and the beach, Bamburgh is a fairly visitor-oriented village. There is no shortage of accommodation or food, although you will look long and hard for boutique hotels or fusion cuisine.

At the homelier end of the scale, the Greenhouse (01668 214513, www.the greenhouseguesthouse.co.uk), on the main street, is a family-run B&B with four decent rooms. The proprietors use organic and Fairtrade produce where possible, and won't flinch when you ask for a vegetarian breakfast.

On the same street, the imposing and flag-bedecked Victoria Hotel (01668 214431, www.victoriahotelbamburgh.net) is a more formal, upmarket operation. The bedrooms are smart and many have four-poster beds; there is also a bar and the Brasserie, a handy, serviceable and busy restaurant.

Down at Seahouses, meanwhile, the not-actually-in-Bamburgh Bamburgh Castle Hotel (01665 720283, www.bamburghcastlehotel.co.uk) has friendly staff, an inn-like atmosphere, some four-poster beds and a harbour view. Many of the bedrooms have sea views, as does the cosy lounge with log fireplace.

For food, Blackett's of Bamburgh (01668 214714) is first choice in this region for its interesting bistro-style menu, while the Copper Kettle Tea Rooms (01688 214361) is a great place for a cosy cream tea when the wind has whipped you raw; the garden is a pretty place for a cuppa when the sun shines. Otherwise, just look for signs advertising local kippers and Bamburgh bangers.

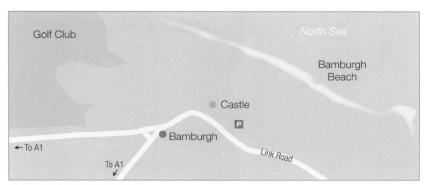

HOW TO GET THERE

By car Turn off the A1 near the village of Belford and take the B1342 east. Part of the National Cycle Network (www.sustrans.org.uk) meanders through this part of the Northumbrian coast and passes through Bamburgh. **By train** Nearest stations are at Berwick-upon-Tweed (18 miles north) and Alnmouth (18 miles south) on the East Coast Mainline. **By bus** Limited local bus services. There are links to Berwick-upon-Tweed and Newcastle-upon-Tyne (0871 200 2233, www.traveline.org.uk,).

PARKING

Pay car park.

FACILITIES

Cafés/restaurant, at castle or in village.Toilets (disabled).

SPORTS

Fishing. Horseriding (Slate Hall Riding Centre, 01665 720320). Surfing.

Windsurfing (for all water sports, bring your own equipment).

SWIMMING

People do swim here, but the summer surface temperature peaks at 14°C. No lifeguard/emergency facilities. RNLI lifeboat station in Seahouses (covers Bamburgh). Water quality: MCS recommended.

RULES

No camping. Barbecues and bonfires permitted (no designated areas, but keep away from the dunes). Dogs permitted (dog bins are provided).

FURTHER REFERENCE

Berwick-upon-Tweed Tourist Information Centre (01289 330733, www.berwick-upon-tweed.gov.uk/guide). Seahouses Tourist Information Centre (01665 720884). Local council (01289 330044, www.berwick-upon-tweed.gov.uk). Website: www.lindisfarne.org.uk.

Barafundle Bay

Fairy tales can come true.

Wales may be synonymous with choirs, miners, valleys and rugby, but once it was a land with a rich tradition of fairy tales. And Barafundle Bay, on the south Pembrokeshire coast, is a good setting for one. In fact, the word 'enchanting' was probably invented for places like this. The approach, for instance, is magical: you must travel along dark, winding forest roads, where the sunlight dances through a canopy of trees. Then there's a cosy village, complete with storybook thatched inn. A homely tea room flanks the entrance to the beach path. And then, after a hike across green and pleasant fields, comes the pièce de resistance: a dainty stone archway, followed by a sweeping stone staircase down to the beach: an entrance grand enough for a princess. As for the sandy main attraction, it is small, secretive and golden – the stuff of childhood memories and family picnics (indeed, *Country Life* magazine recently named it Britain's best beach for just such an activity). Twee? Unashamedly. But be warned: once you pass through the arch, Barafundle casts a spell that is hard to break.

From above, Barafundle is mesmerising. Even in overcast weather, the golden sands emit a curious glow. And the place is often deserted – a ripe setting for an encounter with some fantastical otherworldy creature.

But it is the cosiness of the scene that leaves the biggest impression. Nestled snugly between two limestone headlands, and backed by dunes, Barafundle is a true safe haven. Beyond the headlands, the waves crash angrily against menacing rocks – and bad things happen. Not here. The beach is sheltered from the prevailing south-westerly winds and the surf is gentle (leave your boards at home). The turquoise waters entice and the sugary sandy bottom is easy on the feet.

Sheltered from the open sea, with soft sands and clean waters, Barafundle Bay is a good swimming beach.

On the far side of the beach, on the forested southern fringe, a woodland path lined with sycamore trees again calls to mind children's stories. Behind the dunes, rabbits hop around; more entertainment for the family picnic.

The only thing missing from the storybook scene is a castle, but a Georgian manor house stood here until the 1960s (the Stackpole Estate, on which Barafundle is located, was the lavish property of the Earl of Cawdor in the 18th century; it is now owned by the National Trust).

Even from the loftiest lookout point – the tip of the southern headland – the vista is sweet and serene, rather than staggering: Beachy Head this ain't.

If you leave the safe haven, things get more exciting: beyond the woodland, the Pembrokeshire Coastal Path is exposed, windswept and dramatic. But once you've braved the elements, there's another charm offensive: the Bosherton Lily ponds (an hour's walk from Barafundle). Built in the 18th century by the Earl, these real-life landscape paintings evoke images of frogs and princes, ugly ducklings and swans. You can meander along the pathways, crossing scenic bridges and lingering at lookout points. Otters live here, but you're more likely to see toads, dragonflies or birdlife (swans, kingfisher and herons).

Serious birders will have to go further afield to Stack Rocks, which jut out of the sea near Castlemartin, further west along the coast. In the spring and summer, the rocks swarm with nesting guillemots and razorbills. They compete for airspace with kittiwakes, fulmars and gulls. The sight is hypnotising, and the Green Bridge of Wales, a limestone arch seen from the viewing platform, is similarly weird and wizardly.

There's more mystery and romance at St Govan's Chapel (back east along the coastal path towards Bosherton): this 13th-century hermit's dwelling is hidden in the cliff face at the bottom of 74 steps. Outside there is an ancient wishing well; inside, a haven where St Govan hid from pirates back in the sixth century. It's a majestic spot, what with the waves crashing in and the climbers tackling the cliffs of St Govan's Head above. The lyrical spell is broken, however, by grim, modern reality: the surrounding area is closed for much of the week owing to the presence of a Ministry of Defence firing range (weekends and evenings are your best bet for access, but call 01646 662336/662287 to check path opening times before you set off on your journey).

So when the guns start firing and the birds start squawking, exit the real world and make your way back to Barafundle, out of harm's way. True, dark forces – in the form of mass tourism – threaten the happy ending. After *Country Life*'s Barafundle exposé, the beach's best-kept secret status was blown out of the water. But you can still have the place to yourself off-season, on an overcast day or just on some enchanted evening. So step under the archway onto the golden sands – and let the fairies work their magic.

OTHER BEACHES

Broadhaven, the next beach along, is like Barafundle on steroids. The basics are the same: a shimmering carpet of firmly packed golden sand accessed by way of nature trails. But the canvas is wider and the elements are wilder – it lacks Barafundle's sheltered position. At low tide, the sheer expanse of sand and sky is invigorating.

Freshwater West is only a 20-minute drive west from Barafundle, but the contrast couldn't be greater. The gentle ripples of Barafundle are giant swells here. The picnicking families give way to serious surfer dudes, the cute cove is replaced by a sweeping strand and the sand is often smothered by pebbles and rocks. There's no lifeguard, and no peace: the roar of the surf is relentless.

Manorbier, east along the coast towards Tenby, resembles Barafundle, but is more exposed, with bigger surf, and has more rock pools. It is backed by a Norman castle.

Long a favourite with Northerners and the Welsh, and once a booming Victorian resort, Tenby is largely a forgotten seaside gem, overshadowed in recent years by trendier southern rivals. This is a shame – or perhaps a saving grace. Off the beaten track on the Pembrokeshire coast, Tenby quietly combines class and beauty with a salty, jaunty British seaside feel. The cliff-top promenade, by South Beach, is a study in elegance: a string of smart Georgian buildings painted in pastel shades; old-fashioned street lamps, benches and wrought-iron railings; and tasteful landscaped gardens. The beaches are impeccable – long, firm, and golden – and the harbour is handsome and snug. There's history too, in the form of old city walls, a ruined castle and an ancient monastery across the water on Caldey Island. And yet, despite its pedigree, Tenby has no airs and graces. In contrast to, say, Brighton or Cornwall, boutique hotels, celebrity restaurants and gastropubs are conspicuous by their absence. You won't catch Norman Cook DJing on the beach here. And foodies might go hungry. For purists, though, Tenby is traditional and unpretentious: an irresistible slice of faded seaside grandeur.

WHERE TO STAY AND EAT

With its ivy-covered stone walls, gabled windows and sweet garden, the 17th-century Stackpole Inn (01646 672324, www.stackpoleinn.co.uk) is quaintness writ large. But the four bedrooms are cool and contemporary. The area's best local grub is offered downstairs. Served in a modern rustic setting, the food comprises classy gastropub fare, with fresh local ingredients – Welsh Black beef steaks, Welsh cheeses, Tenby crab, Pembroke sausages – and a selection of real ales.

Set in leafy woodland, about a mile from the coast, the Stackpole Centre (01646 661359, www.nationaltrust.co.uk) is a good base for walking. The converted stone outbuildings and cottages are now comfortable self-catering flats for groups and families.

The Old Smithy B&B (01646 622388) lives up to its characterful name. It's a 200-year-old cottage, with low beamed ceilings, exposed brickwork and antique furniture, complemented by shiny modern bathrooms. It's a ten-minute drive from Barafundle Bay.

St Govan's Country Inn (01646 661311), over in Bosherton, is a down-to-earth, unintentionally retro country pub (swirly red carpets, sports trophies, easy-listening music). It offers no-nonsense grub and rooms (floral bedspreads yes; designer sheets, no).

The sweeping staircase down to the beach adds to the storybook charm.

If you're a beach bum by day and a lady of the manor by night, Portclew House (01646 672800, www.portclewhouse.co.uk) is a grand Georgian country pile right beside Freshwater East beach, and a ten-minute drive from Barafundle.

The Boathouse Tea Room (01646 672058, www.nationaltrust.org.uk, open Easter-Oct, sometimes after Christmas), on tiny Stackpole Harbour, has summery interior decor and outdoor seating. There's a homespun atmosphere, reflected in the food, from ploughman's lunches to cakes galore; it also serves a range of Welsh ales. In summer, it's open in the evenings.

Ye Olde World Café (01646 661216), in Bosherton, suits the area: it's very twee. A quaint little doll's house of a place, it is filled with doilies and dainty antique furniture, with an old-fashioned menu to match – cakes, scones, sandwiches and tea.

Tenby combines smart Georgian architecture, pristine beaches and a snug harbour.

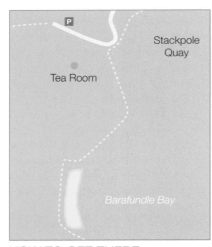

HOW TO GET THERE

By car From Pembroke, take the B4319 south and follow signs to Stackpole village and the Pembrokeshire Coast National Park. Drive through the village, and follow signs to Stackpole Quay and the National Trust Visitor Centre. To get to Stack Rocks, stay on the B4319 to Castlemartin and look for the car park. **By train** Pembroke station is a 20-minute drive. **By bus** The Coastal Cruiser bus runs between Pembroke, Stackpole and Broadhaven (www.pembrokeshire greenways.co.uk). Also try the Green Dragon dial-a-ride bus (www.prta.co.uk).

PARKING

Pay parking, NT members free with card.

FACILITIES

Learning Centre (01646 661464). National Trust Visitor Centre (01646 661359, www.nationaltrust.org.uk). Toilets (disabled).

SPORTS

Climbing (leaflets available from St Govan's Inn and Visitor Centre).

SWIMMING

No lifeguard or emergency facilities. Coast guard (01646 690909). Water quality: MCS recommended. Green Coast Award.

RULES

No barbecues or fires. Dogs permitted.

FURTHER REFERENCE

Pembrokeshire Tourist Information (01646 622388, visitpembrokeshire. com). Pembrokeshire Coast National Park (0845 345 7275, www. pembrokeshirecoast.org.uk). Local council (www.pembrokeshire.gov.uk). Website: www.pcnpa.org.uk.

Rhossili Bay

A view to a thrill.

The Gower peninsula, in the south-west corner of Wales, was the first place in Britain to be designated an Area of Outstanding Natural Beauty. But Rhossili Bay, the region's showpiece, should receive an award for best drama. If you've come in search of cosy coves, gentle paddling and seaside jollity, move along – or get serious. This is the landscape of the sublime. The beach gives new meaning to the word sweeping; the thundering surf is relentless; the dunes (and downs) are mountainous; and the wind can whip you raw. On a stormy day, this is Wales at its wettest and wildest. You are at the mercy of the elements, and the Atlantic – there's nothing between here and America – throws everything it can at you. Yet, above all, it is the view that really stirs the soul. The scene from above could compete with the some of the world's most famous coastal vistas: the US Highway 1 in California, say, or Australia's Great Ocean Road.

Though the Gower won its natural beauty designation back in 1963, the news has been slow to catch on. On a sunny summer Saturday, for instance, the beach can be deserted. This is partly down to scale: Rhossili's vastness (it is three miles long and, at low tide, feels about three miles wide) means you will never be jostling for towel space. But you may never want to bring a towel: the wind can be merciless (sunbathers take refuge behind windbreaks here) and the swimming can be treacherous. The water is frigid and, when the surf is strong, there can be a dangerous undertow.

The Atlantic swells may deter swimmers, but they attract surfers by the VW-vanload. The northern corner, Llangennith, often resembles a colony of human seals, with a sea of black wetsuits filling the horizon. At the end of the day, the surfers congregate in the hills above at the King's Head pub in Llangennith village, talking about break points like Welsh Keanu Reeveses. The stiff breezes also lure hang gliders, paragliders and kite-flyers.

But these are bit players in Rhossili's cast of characters: walkers play the main role. This beach was made for walking: it is long, wide and firmly packed and the crashing surf is a soundtrack for soul searching. Still, many walkers don't even set foot on the beach. For one thing, it's a long walk down; for another, Rhossili makes the biggest impact from above. In fact, the money shot (the curving sweep of beach looking north) can be captured from the terrace of the Worm's Head Hotel, pint in hand, without breaking a sweat.

Still, most people head for the hills. The name Rhossili is derived from the Welsh word *Rhos*, for moorland. And the scene along the Downs paths – gorse, heather, sheep, a lone stone cottage – is classic Welsh pastoral. In true Enid Blyton style, many walkers lie down in the heather, while anoraks dig around for the Iron Age remains and a ruined World War II radar station. Romantics, meanwhile, ponder a reclusive life at the Old Rectory, a lonely hillside cottage (it is available to rent).

But thoughts of lonely shepherds are drowned out by the ocean's roar, and the jaw-dropping spectacle beneath you. Cameras go crazy here and one of the classic photographs is of Worm's Head. The Vikings thought it looked like a dragon or 'Wurm', but this curiously shaped peninsula calls to mind the Loch Ness monster. It's certainly scary getting there: you can only cross to the Head at low tide and then must come back within two hours or be stranded.

Twitchers might not mind: the Head is swarming with razorbills, kittiwakes, fulmars, cormorants and, from April to July, puffins. But don't get too entranced: not for nothing is the rocky causeway between the mainland and the Head called 'Devil's Bridge'. Every year, somebody drowns or needs rescuing – even Dylan Thomas got trapped here for an evening, and wrote about it in his short story 'Who Do You Think Was With Us?' In 1932, a flock of 70 sheep was swept away while attempting to make the crossing.

The greatest human tragedy occurred in 1887, when a Norwegian ship was wrecked just beyond the Head during a fierce November storm. The decayed hull of the *Helvetia*

Paragliders are out in
force when the wind is
blowing; walkers are a
presence in all weathers.

still pokes evocatively through the sand at the south end of the beach – a poignant reminder of Rhossili's elemental grandeur. A greater calamity occurred 500 years previously, when the original village of Rhossili was buried by the sand in a storm.

The current village was wisely built on the top of the cliffs. On a stormy day, it resembles a tiny, forlorn frontier community: man against the elements. But in summer, the place becomes a living, breathing postcard. No wonder the new village was placed above. Its builders knew what subsequent walkers, photographers and romantics have discovered: getting high is the best way to appreciate Rhossili.

OTHER BEACHES

Broughton Bay, round the corner from Rhossili on the Gower's north shore, is another big, bold and beautiful beach, backed by large dunes. Off the beaten path, it rarely gets crowded. But if Rhossili is occasionally dodgy for swimming, Broughton Bay is downright treacherous; its tides can be fearsome. Surfers, however, are not deterred.

Port Eynon, on the south-western corner of the Gower, is the region's grittiest beach – in more ways than one. The sand can be mucky, covered in seaweed and rocks. Caravan parks and campsites abound. And the village pub is just plain rough. But this beach has a down-to-earth appeal. It's a hive of activity, with watersports galore, a lifeguard in the summer and a chippie on the front. The swimming is safe, if you don't get run over by a jet-ski, and the water quality is better here than at Rhossili (it is MCS recommended and has also been awarded a Blue Flag). The dunes backing the mile-long beach are enormous, and there's a lovely boardwalk through them.

Mewslade Bay, a rugged hike along the coast from Worm's Head, offers striking views of the Head. Remote and deserted, it has the air of a best-kept secret. The craggy cliffs and virgin sands are seductive, but don't swim here in strong surf; there's an undertow.

The Gower does not have a monopoly on the region's best beaches. Cefn Sidan, about an hour's drive north in Carmarthenshire, is the biggest beach in Wales: a staggering seven miles long. The wide, pancake-flat sand lures kite buggies and walkers, who also frequent the nature trails in the pine forest. Swimming is safe within designated areas, but be warned – it's a long walk to the water's edge. *See also pp184-191.*

WHERE TO STAY AND EAT

The location of the Worm's Head Hotel (01792 390512, www.thewormshead.co.uk), on the edge of Rhossili's famous lookout point, is worth the price alone. The 24 rooms, though not the height of fashion, all have sea views. Food is solid pub fare (Welsh lamb, seafood, comforting desserts) served in the bar, restaurant or terrace, with stupendous views in all.

The King's Head pub (01792 386212, www.kingsheadgower.co.uk) in Llangennith may be filled with surfers, but the bedrooms – with chocolate bedlinen and plasma TVs – are positively chic for these parts. The best food in Llangennith is to be found here: the chalkboard menu is by turns adventurous and comforting, from a medley of Thai dishes (a speciality) to liver and bacon casserole, complemented by irresistible puddings.

The lonely Old Rectory cottage, perched romantically above the sea on the Rhossili Downs, can be rented (0870 458 4422, www.nationaltrustcottages.co.uk).

Further afield, there is accommodation and sophisticated dining in Oxwich Bay (*see pp184-191*). The Port Eynon Youth Hostel (0870 770 8868, www.yha.org.uk) combines character (it's set in an old lifeboat station) with location (the ocean is on its doorstep).

Next door to the Worm's Head Hotel, the Bay Bistro and Coffee House (01792 390519) has the same magnificent view and serves fresh and local seafood.

Stretching for three shimmering miles, Rhossili is made for bare feet; above right, the wreck of the *Helvetia*.

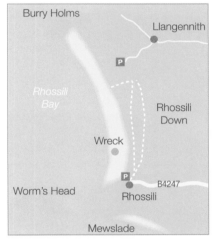

HOW TO GET THERE

By car From Swansea, take the A4118 and follow the signs to the Gower peninsula. Once on the peninsula, follow signs towards Port Eynon. Then take the B4247 to Rhossili. **By bus** The Gower Explorer 118 from Swansea's central bus station goes to Rhossili (0871 200 2233, www.traveline-cymru.org.uk).

PARKING

Pay parking at Rhossili and Llangennith.

FACILITIES

Hotel. National Trust Centre (April-Oct, 01792 390707, www.nationaltrust.org).

Pub. Shop. Toilets (in the villages, not on the beach).

SPORTS

Horse riding (Pilton Moor Stables, Rhossili, 01792 390554). Kite boarding (Gower Kite Riders, 01792 367453, www.gowerkiteriders.com). Surfing (PJ's Surf Shop, Llangennith, 01792 386669, www.pjsurfshop.co.uk; Sam's Surf Shack Board & Wetsuit Hire, Rhossili, at the back of Bay Bistro, 01792 390519).

SWIMMING

Do not bathe in strong surf due to undertow, particularly at Llangennith end. The south end of the beach is more sheltered and there are no rip currents, but exercise caution. No lifeguard. Water standard: EC Guideline.

RULES

No bonfires or barbecues. No camping. Dogs allowed, but must be on lead at lambing time (around March).

FURTHER REFERENCE

Swansea Tourist Information (01792 468321). Local council (01792 636000, www.swansea.gov.uk). Websites: www.enjoygower.com; www.visitwales.co.uk.

Oxwich Bay

In a class of its own.

Oxwich Bay has a big reputation to live up to. In 2007, the Welsh beauty made headlines across the country when it was voted Britain's best beach by a glossy travel magazine. In the same survey, which inspected 1,000 beaches across the globe, this quiet strand finished in the world's top 12, beating more famous competitors from California to the Caribbean.

At first glance, however, the hype seems misleading. Sure, Oxwich is pretty, but there are more visually impressive beaches elsewhere on the Gower peninsula; dramatic Rhossili Bay (*see p176*), for instance, or secluded Three Cliffs Bay. But Oxwich is probably the best all-rounder. For while Rhossili Bay is spectacular, its wild and windy setting means a day at the beach is, well, not exactly a day at the beach. And while Three Cliffs is impossibly romantic, the reality is less alluring: it's a schlep to get there, there are no creature comforts and the swimming is not safe.

Oxwich, by contrast, manages the rare feat of combining sweeping scenery – more than two curvaceous miles of pale sands – with accessibility. This is a beach for those who like their beauty without cruelty, who like a contemplative walk instead of a rugged hike, who like their solitude within easy reach of supplies.

Indeed, where Rhossili is staggering and dramatic, Oxwich is kind and gentle – and easier on the senses. On some days, a gale might be blowing at the former, forcing sunbathers to huddle behind windbreaks. But at the same time, just around the corner, sheltered Oxwich might be kissed by a sea breeze.

The terrain is softer too. Instead of the lonely, windswept downs of Rhossili, Oxwich is backed by green hills and verdant forests. The dunes also seem smaller. Even the nature reserve, behind the dunes, is somehow more benign: whereas Rhossili's windswept downs are synonymous with scrappy heather, here there are fragile orchids, butterflies and lizards. Twitchers, meanwhile, can ogle a stellar cast – whitethroat, sedge warbler, reed bunting, white heron and little egret – without getting blown off their feet. And swimmers can bathe in relative safety: the water is shallow and calm compared to its surfing cousin (though there is no lifeguard).

All is not complete bliss, however. The boats and jet-skis are a menace to both swimmers (steer clear of the slipway) and soul searchers. The busy west side of the beach verges on the unsightly: the car park is a blight on the horizon; the concrete toilets and

kiosks are eyesores; and the sand is pockmarked with stones and seaweed. On a hot day, the crowds of families and the roar of the jet-skis shatter the tranquility. Here, it is hard to believe that Oxwich beat Oahu.

But walk east, towards Tor Bay and Three Cliffs, and it's a different world. The crowds dissipate, the sand smooths out and the shoes come off. Or the bikes come out – at low tide, the sand is so flat and firmly packed that cyclists can virtually fly down the length of the beach. But they are outnumbered by walkers. This is the kind of pristine sand that cries out for bare feet. Footprints here are left by couples strolling, children frolicking and lads playing frisbee. There are usually a few paw prints too (dog walking is permitted all year). In fact, bare feet are advisable if you want to walk the entire length of the beach: halfway down there is a tidal stream to cross.

Ironically, as you leave the crowds behind, the scenery improves. By Tor Bay, the dunes give way to craggy postcard scenery. One postcard in particular comes to mind: Three Cliffs Bay, the poster child of the Gower peninsula, pictured in every travel feature about South Wales. If the scenery looks familiar, that's because you are looking at the real thing: Three Cliffs is Oxwich's next-door neighbour. At low tide, you can walk around the cliffs to the famous bay and see what all the fuss is about. But don't go swimming there: behind the beauty is a treacherous undertow.

At this end of the beach, you could be at the edge of the world. But civilisation is never far away at Oxwich. Back at the west end, the kiosk sells everything from buckets and spades to sun cream, baseball caps to sausage rolls. Entertainment comes in the form of wakeboarding and waterskiing, kayaking or kite-surfing, banana boats and doughnut rides. The village shop sells tabloids, the Oxwich Bay Hotel provides sustenance beyond Cornettos, and a woodland walk to Oxwich Point – past a medieval church and a 16th-century manor house, Oxwich Castle – satisfies nature lovers and culture vultures.

Suddenly, you start to see why Oxwich is a world beater. It may not inspire love at first sight, like Three Cliffs Bay, or offer staggering vistas, as does Rhossili, but it is a bona fide people pleaser. It's got the beauty spot credentials, but you can also swim, play, walk, shop, think, eat, drink and be merry – and then hop in the car without having to endure an epic hike, plane journey or tropical disease. You can't do all that in Bora Bora.

OTHER BEACHES

You've seen Three Cliffs Bay before. On the cover of books, travel magazines and, most recently, as a finalist on ITV's *Britain's Favourite Views* programme. Campers know about it too, as the hills above boast the most scenic pitch in the country. The publicity should have ruined the place. And yet, on a warm summer day, Three Cliffs can still be deserted. What the postcards don't say is that the swimming is not great here, owing to the undertow. Or that it's a bit of a hike to get here, albeit a pleasant one, through woodland and a valley overlooked by a ruined castle, then across an ankle-deep tidal stream. Or that the facilities are non-existent. But the postcards don't lie about the craggy scenery, the natural arches and caves, the vast canvas of white sands and sheer magic of the place. For once, the reality lives up to the great expectations.

For more beaches in the Gower peninsula and South Wales, *see pp176-183*.

On the south side of the Gower, and protected by a headland, Oxwich is more sheltered than Rhossili, its wild neighbour.

WHERE TO STAY AND EAT

A room with a view is the best reason to stay at Oxwich Bay Hotel (01792 390329, www.oxwichbayhotel.co.uk), the only hotel next to the beach. The rooms are on the frumpy side, but location trumps fashion here. The restaurant feels a bit plush 1970s, with red velvet, mirrored walls and easy rock on the stereo, but the wide-reaching menu varies from hearty pub grub to more ambitious fare, and it beats the beach kiosk.

On a hill above Oxwich, Penrice Castle Cottages (01792 391212, www.penrice castle.co.uk) are literally a cut above. The cottages are in the grounds of a ruined medieval castle, and many have gardens and sea views.

Further afield, in Reynoldston, the King Arthur Hotel (01792 390775, www.king arthurhotel.co.uk) has 19 rooms, tastefully done up with sturdy wooden furniture and brass beds. It's best known for its gastropub and restaurant, though. The decor is cosy

Oxwich Church and the adjacent woodland offer physical and spiritual shelter.

country inn personified, the staff are young and sexy, and there's lots of locally caught seafood and fresh meat (Welsh steak and lamb) on the blackboard menu, plus banoffee pie for dessert. The beach is a 15-minute drive.

Three Cliffs Bay Holiday Park (01792 371218, www.threecliffsbay.com) offers camping, caravan and cottage facilities – and one of the most famous views in the Gower.

Deep in the countryside, the elegant Fairyhill Hotel is the top of the Gower crop. In an old ivy-covered stately home, the luxurious rooms are done up in dark green to match the woodland setting, with 21st-century flourishes (Wi-Fi, DVDs). The restaurant is pure class, a serene and sophisticated place overlooking a garden; the menu draws foodies from miles around. For more accommodation in the Gower, *see p182*.

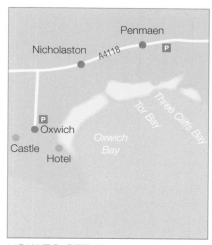

SPORTS

Boating. Canoeing. Horse riding (Pilton Moor Stables, Rhossili, 01792 390554). Kayaking. Kitesurfing. Sailing (Euphoria Sailing, 01792 234502, www.euphoria sailing.com, www.watersports4all.com). Scuba diving. Surfing. Wakeboarding. Windsurfing.

SWIMMING

Good for swimming; lifeguard in the summer holidays only, watch out for the occasional jellyfish. Emergency facilities. Don't swim by slipway. Undertow at Three Cliffs Bay, do not swim there. Water quality: MCS recommended.

HOW TO GET THERE

By car From Swansea, take the A4118 to the Gower peninsula. Follow the road past Killay and turn left at sign for Oxwich. The car park is at the end of the road. **By bus** Gower Explorer 117 bus runs every two hours from Swansea's Quadrant bus station to Oxwich (0871 200 2233, www.traveline-cymru.org.uk).

RULES

Barbecues and fires permitted only with written permission from Penrice Castle Estate Office (01792 391081). Dogs permitted (on leads). No horse riding April-Sept.

FURTHER REFERENCE

Swansea Tourist Information (01792 468321). Local council: (01792 636000, www.swansea.gov.uk). Websites: www.enjoygower.com; www.the-gower.com; www.thislandwales.com; www.visitswanseabay.com;

PARKING

Pay parking.

FACILITIES

Phone booths. Restaurant. Shops. Toilets (disabled).

Hell's Mouth

Wet, wild and Welsh.

On a shimmering, sunny day – you do get them in North Wales – Hell's Mouth would seem a misnomer. Why, it even won a Green Coast award for all-round fabulousness from the Welsh Assembly in 2007. This beach is not always so inviting, however. When the wind off the Atlantic starts its infernal howling, whipping up the breakers and snatching the boards from the purpled hands of surfers, the wide-mouthed bay on the end of the Lleyn peninsula becomes the devil's own strand.

This hellish reputation comes from its shipwrecking tendencies, evidence of which lies deep under the sod in the churchyard at Llanengan (the nearest village) – although, in fact, there may be a more benign reason for the name, as 'hell' in ancient Norse means 'clear'. The sea is clean, if not limpid, and this lack of pollution is one reason why wildlife spotters often see porpoises passing through.

The Welsh name for the bay is Porth Neigwl, after nobleman Nigel de Loryng. Back in the 14th century, de Loryng was given this parcel of land by the Black Prince, eldest son of Edward III.

Little remains of the township, Neigwl, that de Loryng set up to keep the Welsh peasantry working their jerkins off for him, but much has been written about the wreckers of Hell's Mouth. Although the setting of false lights on rocky coastlines was a lucrative practice all over the British coastline in centuries past, few bays were as notorious as Hell's Mouth. The bloodiest event took place in 1629, when a French ship carrying noblemen and women was lured on to the rocks and the wreckers invaded the vessel, murdering and maiming the unfortunate passengers while relieving them of valuables. Schooners were still getting into difficulties here well into the 20th century.

Even today, ships give the area a wide berth. And the occasionally tricky cross-currents and strong undertows can make it a challenging swim. Surfers, on the other hand, appreciate its position, facing south-west. They may be scathing about summer waves, but in the autumn, strong winds and eight-foot swells turn the sea into a cauldron.

Many say the northern end of the beach is best for experienced surfers, as the steep, barrelling waves bounce off the cliffs with a mighty thump. On blowy days, beginner surfers are happiest at Bwlchtocyn, the south-eastern end.

Come on a still summer's day, however, and the beach is as tame a beast as you're likely to play frisbee on. Families with people-carrier-loads of UV-resistant tents, bodyboards, windbreakers, lilos and beach balls set up camp in one of the sandy inlets among the shallow dunes, where beach meets sheep fields. Before you find an isolated spot to set up camp (not difficult), you negotiate an area of flotsam and jetsam kicked up the beach. This rubbish is disappointing, given the water's squeaky-clean reputation, but it is one of the disadvantages of such splendid isolation (there are no dustbins, so a few brain-dead trippers don't clean up after themselves).

Litter notwithstanding, Hell's Mouth is a heavenly spot. It's flanked by headlands of rare beauty – both gifts to walkers. To the north is Mynydd Penarfynydd, near Rhiw, where peregrine falcons and Cornish choughs (chased away from Cornwall by the crowds, it seems) wheel around the rocky outcrops. The southern headland, known as Mynydd Gilan, is equally scenic, although seasoned walkers favour the more deserted Rhiw end.

Between these is the glorious sandy strand – about four miles – where, on cloudless days, a lack of shade can be a problem. There's no lack of sand, though, and nicely varied it is too: some firm and flat for beach games, with softer stuff for digging and building. There are also seaweedy rock pools for crab hunting and scrambling upon.

On the horizon, Bardsey Island provides a focal point for gazing. Purportedly a burial place for 20,000 saints, today it is a place of pilgrimage for nature lovers.

You can reach Bardsey by boat from Aberdaron, at the tip of the peninsula. Bardsey Sound, which separates the two, is notoriously turbulent: indeed, it is responsible for as many wrecks as Hell's Mouth. Legend has it that King Arthur's ship, *Caswennan*, was smashed up on the island's rocks. The boat trip, and the chance to swim near seals or bottlenose dolphins and hear the cries of a thousand seabirds, is an adventure. So inspiring is Bardsey, you can almost believe the legend of the monks who lived to saintly ages, thanks to the island's healing properties. They were probably just thankful they made it safely across Bardsey Sound – and away from the mouth of Hell.

Hidden in the wilds of North Wales, Hell's Mouth is still unspoiled, and has won a Green Coast award for its conservation efforts.

OTHER BEACHES

Posh Abersoch, on the east coast of the Lleyn peninsula, is the Welsh answer to Cornwall's Rock. Its three beaches are all busy in high season, drawing designer-clad boardriders, jet-skiers and kite-surfers, who are well set up with cafés, loos and ice-cream vendors.

Of the beautiful beaches bookending Hell's Mouth, the tiny Porth Ysgo, at the western end, is wild and gorgeous, but has no facilities to speak of. Instead, there are rocks, sand at low tide, a tumbling stream, steep cliffs all around and remnants of mining machinery crumbling picturesquely. You get to it via 100 steps. It's a diamond among beaches, and the huge boulders are beloved of climbers, but it's probably not one for

HOW TO GET THERE

By car From Pwllheli, take the A499 to Abersoch and then follow the signs to Llanengan. Go through the village, follow the brown signs (*traeth* means beach). Park on the road or in the free car park.
By bus There is a bus from Pwllheli to Llanengan. (0871 200 2233, www. traveline-cymru.org.uk). The latter is a 15-minute walk from the beach For day trips to Bardsey Island, board the ferry at Porth Meudwy, near Aberdaron (0845 811 3655/07836 293146, www.enllicharter.co.uk).

PARKING
Free.

FACILITIES
Ice-cream van (seasonal). Surf van (selling surf accessories).

SPORTS
Horse riding (school and Lusitano stud at Llaniestyn, 01758 730741, www.lusitano cymru.co.uk). Surfing (Offaxis Wakeboard and Surf Academy, 01758 713407, www.offaxis.co.uk). Wakeboarding (Europe's largest wakeboarding competition, Wakestock, is held every July at Abersoch, www. wakestock.co.uk).

SWIMMING
No lifeguard. Emergency facilities/phone. Water quality: MCS recommended. Green Coast Award.

RULES
No barbecues, bonfires or camping. Dogs permitted (no bins).

FURTHER REFERENCE
Abersoch Tourist Information (01758 712929). North Wales Tourism (01492 531731, www.nwt.co.uk). Pwllheli Tourist Information (01758 613000). Local council (www.gwynedd.gov.uk). Websites: www.gonorthwales.co.uk; www.westcoastsurf.co.uk.

young children. Porth Ceiriad, Porth Ysgo's brother-in-charms on the south-eastern side of Hell's Mouth, is a sheltered beach, with more cliffs and challenging surf. Again, it's remote and has no café or loos. You park at Nant-y-Big farm and take steep steps down.

If you want a family-friendly beach, but can't take trendy Abersoch, go west to Aberdaron. The pretty town – a muddle of stone cottages – leads to a wide sandy beach with lots of facilities. Aberdaron is associated with Wales' other renowned poet, RS Thomas, who lived here. He had little time for the English, however much they loved his beach.

WHERE TO STAY AND EAT

Happy campers will find any number of sites in the Abersoch/Llanengan area. Treheli, a farm at Rhiw (01758 780281), has astounding views of Hell's Mouth, and is the closest site to the beach. The manicured green of Glanmorfa campsite, near Llanengan (open May-August, 01758 712965), is well equipped and well positioned.

More solid accommodation comes by way of Ty'N Don (01286 831184, www.tyndon.co.uk), a cliff-top farm overlooking Hell's Mouth, with private access. Some of its simple self-catering cottages have sea views. Another back-to-basics option is a bunkhouse on the Tanrallt family farm in Llangian (01758 713527), a mile from the beach.

The poshest hotel on the Peninsula is Porth Tocyn Hotel, aloof in the hills above Abersoch (01758 713303, www.porth-tocyn-hotel.co.uk). Praised by generations of families, this family-run establishment is like a rich old auntie's farmhouse by the sea. Furnishings are shabby chic and tasteful, and there are splendid gardens, tennis courts and an outdoor pool. Meals are wonderfully lavish, but booking is essential.

If it's austerity and wilderness you crave, there are cottages for hire by the week on Bardsey Island (08458 112233, www.bardsey.org).

The Sun Inn, the local Robinsons pub, at Llanengan (01758 712660), offers the only meals at Hell's Mouth. It's pleasant and reasonably priced, but won't bowl over foodies.

The other eating choices are in upmarket Abersoch. The people's favourite is Mañana (01758 713144), a Mexican place where they don't take bookings, so queues of fajita-starved teens are common in summer. Another winner is Angelina's (01758 712353, www.angelinas.co.uk), where the pizzas are terrific and the meat and fish reassuringly local.

Hell's Mouth is famous among surfers, but the rolling countryside on the Lleyn peninsula is largely undiscovered by tourists.

Calgary

Senses working overtime.

Arran has accessibility, Islay and Jura whisky, the Outer Hebrides their atmosphere of periphery and Skye has *sturm und drang*. But of all the islands off Scotland's west coast, Mull – and its chorus of historic, geological and scenic dramas – shifts something deep down inside its visitors, like the activation of an extra sense.

On Mull, the familiar recipe of land, sea, and sky arrives on a different frequency. After a few days here, visitors are taken over by the island's rhythm and vibration, from the fast Atlantic wash to the slow life of its mountains. Time stands still here: the people who were cleared from the hamlet of Inivea above Calgary Bay, in the early 19th century, seemingly left yesterday; the rise in sea level that could soon swallow up the coastline seems thousands of years away.

Even amid all the rich scenery, the beach at Calgary is sufficiently remarkable to stand out. The journey there, however, is almost as memorable as the strand itself. The ferry from Oban, the most popular route, deposits passengers at Craignure on the south side of Mull, but it takes no time to reach the north and west. Driving past the shadowy Loch na Keal – an open sea loch on the west coast – the sky deepens, the water is crowded with drowned mountains, and the steep cliffs of Creag Brimishgan and Creag Mhor at the loch's edge loom majestically on the horizon. If something catches your eye, soaring above, it is quite probably a golden eagle. If you are lucky, it might even be a white-tailed sea eagle: rarer than its golden cousin and much larger.

Small and sheltered, Calgary is beloved of families, with a gentle slope for safe splashing and good beachcombing potential.

For another eye-catching diversion, look to the hills: by Loch Tuath, everyone stops to gape at Eas Fors, a series of waterfalls tumbling off the cliffs into the sea. A bit further on, the Treshnish Isles, a mysterious archipelago of uninhabited islands, add to the drama.

The aesthetic sucker punches then stop for a while as you veer inland, before returning to the sea at Calgary Bay – and the most awesome spectacle. As you round the bend in the road, brace yourself for an involuntary gasp. Suddenly, on the horizon, a jewel of a beach comes into view: white gold banded by turquoise, complemented by something semiprecious in darker green and solid igneous surroundings.

Protected by the deep bay and surrounded by low hills, Calgary beach is sheltered and small, but perfectly formed. It only runs only a quarter of a mile from end to end, but is backed by storybook woodland and colourful machair – a rare coastal grassland, covered with wild flowers, and unique to Scotland and Ireland. The water is clean and generally calm, while the slope is gentle, staying shallow for some distance. Hardy people do swim, although the sea surface temperature at the height of summer barely touches 14°C (wetsuits help).

On a typical July day – rain, wind, sunshine – swimming costume-clad children play in the surf, while more transient visitors pull their anorak hoods tight and mature ladies behind windbreaks delve deeper into books. With no immediate diversions, you have to amuse yourself; only picnic tables and a public toilet pay lip-service to the idea of 'facilities'. There is a Georgian mansion – Calgary Castle – but it offers nothing to the public, although its woodland sculpture walk takes you towards the Calgary Hotel.

This is not an ice-cream beach then. There is no guaranteed warmth and no bars, topless sunbathing or men selling trinkets. But on those occasional summer days when the sea is Aegean blue, and the air temperature nudges above 20°C, Calgary acts like a visitor magnet. There could be literally dozens and dozens of people here. Despite its picture perfection, and growing celebrity, for much of the year you can often have the beach to yourself, thanks to the Hebridean climate. That is perhaps the best time to consider it as it once was.

The old burial ground behind the beach, and the ruins of the crofting township of Inivea up a hill on the north side, hint at a slightly more populous era. By modern standards, Mull was never crowded, but it did hit a demographic peak – about 10,000 – in the mid 19th century. Today, fewer than 3,000 people live on the entire island, a process of emigration begun long ago by poverty, famine and eviction. The Calgary Bay crofters were yet another strand in the fabric of loss labelled the Highland Clearances: tenants displaced in favour of sheep.

The people may be gone, but two centuries later the sheep remain, grazing on the machair, while there are cattle nearby too. The very word Calgary derives from the Gaelic cala ghearraidh – 'bay of the pasture' – so animals, and the people who tended them, have walked here for eons.

Did those ancient residents appreciate just how precious Calgary is? It's hard to imagine anyone taking it for granted. In basic beach terms, Calgary is hard to resist: good swimming, lovely shells, pretty jellyfish and immaculate sand. But its charms are more complex. You could be seduced by its prettiness alone, yet deeper souls will step into another dimension of time and savour its fragile beauty. In geological terms, Calgary beach

is an elusive visitor, appearing and disappearing as the sea dictates. Experts say it could slip under the azure waters sometime in the next 100 years. So soak up the scenery – and awaken your senses – while you still can.

Calgary Castle offers fairy-tale accommodation overlooking the beach.

OTHER BEACHES

Unlike many other Hebridean islands, Mull is not blessed with endless sands. If you have travelled all this way, however, and can go that bit further, the other must-see beaches are on Iona next door. Catch the small ferry from Fionnphort at the Ross of Mull, and in just ten minutes you will reach this atmospheric island, walking in the footsteps of Columba, the sixth-century saint. Many people come here to visit the ancient abbey, a cradle of Christianity, but Iona also has a fine coastline, particularly the Bay at the Back of the Ocean, with its dunes and machair. Given Iona's religious associations, some find that this beach aids spiritual contemplation. Others see it in more prosaic, geographical terms: next stop, Newfoundland. Either way, it is beautiful – especially in good light.

WHERE TO STAY AND EAT

Dramatic Calgary Castle offers beds just behind the beach, but is only let in its self-catering entirety and in week-long blocks (01449 741066, www.calgary-castle.com). Prices start at £2,300, which sounds steep, but it holds up to 12 adults plus four children and comes with fishing rights, housekeepers and 40 acres of woods.

The friendly Calgary Hotel (01688 400256, www.calgary.co.uk) is a more affordable option. Though it closes down for much of the winter, it's a beauty, nestled quietly on a

forested hillside. There are a couple of dining options here: a bistro, done up in rustic style, serving local meat and seafood, as well as the Carthouse Gallery, which offers snacks and light lunches and shows local artworks.

Otherwise, you must go inland to Dervaig, which has a few B&Bs and the Bellachroy Inn (01688 400314, www.thebellachroy.co.uk). Dating from 1608, this authentic drovers' inn is the oldest hotel on Mull. Though short on frills, it is big on atmosphere.

Finally, the heaving metropolis of Tobermory has a range of hotels and eateries, best combined at the Highland Cottage (01688 302030, www.highlandcottage.co.uk). The rooms are a mix of traditional furnishings and modern comforts, and many critics deem the dining room, which serves local crabs, mussels and scallops, the best on Mull.

HOW TO GET THERE

By car/ferry Calgary is on the north-west coast of Mull, 12 miles west of Tobermory. Caledonian MacBrayne (www.calmac.co.uk) operates the principal Oban-Craignure route (46-minute crossing), also Kilchoan-Tobermory (35 minutes) and Lochaline-Fishnish (15 minutes). Its website carries details of the very limited community ferry that links Tobermory with Laga and Drimnin on the mainland (foot passengers, bicycles and dogs only) plus the short hop from Mull to Iona. Although there are ferry services from the remote mainland peninsulas north of the island, the majority of visitors arrive from Oban and follow the B8073, via Salen, to Calgary. **By bus** The 494 bus runs a limited service between Tobermory and Calgary (several on weekdays, two on Saturday, none on Sunday; 01688 302220).

PARKING
Free (north end of the bay).

FACILITIES
Picnic tables. Toilets (south end).

SPORTS
Angling (from headlands, for sea trout, mackerel and cod).

SWIMMING
Gentle slope, so good for children. No lifeguards. Water quality: not MCS tested.

RULES
No camping on the beach or machair. Bonfires discouraged. Dogs permitted, but must be controlled to protect sheep.

FURTHER REFERENCE
Craignure Tourist Information (0870 720 0610). Tobermory Tourist Information (April-Oct, 01688 302182). Local council (www.argyll-bute.gov.uk). Website: www.undiscoveredscotland.co.uk.

Luskentyre

Swept away.

Standing in the water at Luskentyre feels a bit like having your first bite of ice-cream. With the frigid North Atlantic lapping at your ankles, and unnaturally white sands all around, you are hit by a burst of sensation: a head-rushing chill combined with giddy pleasure. Physically fresh and visually sublime, this beach is delicious and overwhelming.

Anyone expecting a simple crescent strand will be baffled: at low tide, the entire bay before you becomes a beach. Or rather, a swirling 'complex' of sands, measuring one mile across and about two miles long, cut through by shimmering channels of seawater in 100 shades of blue, and framed by the impossibly ancient hills of the Outer Hebrides.

This unique topography is the first thing you notice when you arrive on the island of Harris. Strange and uneven, faded green and pale grey, it is dotted everywhere with lochans, pools and exposed stones – as if Harris had failed to decide between water and earth. There are mountains (the highest being the 2,630-foot Clisham to the north), but a great sweep of the island's south and east coasts, near the ferry port of Tarbert, is low-lying, stark and alien. On the west coast, Luskentyre (or Losgaintir in the original Gaelic) looks rather different – here, the terrain is modestly mountainous and three-dimensional, with Beinn Dhubh looming almost 2,000 feet above.

Luskentyre may be the name for a minor settlement (comprising a few houses), but it is also a general moniker for several conjoined beaches around the bay. Many people first feel the sand under their feet at Traigh Rosamol, a few miles north of Luskentyre town. The sheer scale of the environment here is giddying. Insistent waves wash the beach smooth, and the sand seems to slide away for untold miles towards unreachable hills, its end point impossible to pin down from pedestrian perspectives. And then you walk into that ice-cream sea and the feeling of exhilaration plays further havoc with your senses.

Rosamol may be tucked round a headland, but you can walk back to Luskentyre from here, light sand and silver-bright surf all the way. Luskentyre beach itself (Traigh Losgaintir) is south and east of the eponymous hamlet, while the south-west corner of the bay has the third star in the sandy triumvirate: Traigh Sheileboist (Seilebost beach), on a finger of land poking north from the settlement of the same name.

For the postcard shot – a view of the full sandy sweep – go further south on the A859, past Seilebost, and look across the mouth of the inlet. There is enough elevation here for a remarkable panorama: cloud-shadowed hills, expansive beach, lapis lazuli water and occasional dark reefs breaching the surface.

Wherever you stand on Harris, the ground underfoot is Lewisian gneiss – at three billion years old, the most antique rock in Europe. Looking at the mystical landscape at Luskentyre, such an incomprehensible span starts to make some sense.

But mostly this island will shake you up and twist your head. The sheer distance travelled to reach the Outer Hebrides unsettles the mental space inhabited by the visitor. The ridiculous proportion of this beach, or beach system, pulls a rug from under you,

The vivid colours and white sands look tropical, but the water temperature is decidedly Scottish.

destroying all traditional perceptions of physical space. Bring time into the equation (that Lewisian gneiss), plus the alien look of the island, and you're lost. Travelling here does not broaden the mind; it reorders it.

Even seasoned travellers are never quite prepared for Luskentyre. Rocks two-thirds as old as the Earth; ancient colours; a tide that ebbs to suddenly reveal square miles of enclosed sands; the roiling mass of the North Atlantic beyond Taransay. It may be fearsome in winter and on grey days, but when the sun shines, Luskentyre reverts to ice-cream fantasy and becomes an accidental Oz.

Magical, tantalising, and very far away.

OTHER BEACHES

The west coast of South Harris is peppered with sandy strips. Once past Seilebost, part of the 'Luskentyre complex', head south-west on the A859. The next six miles of coastline are beach heaven – especially to jaded urban eyes. From the strand and campsite at Horgabost all the way down to the major traigh at Scarista, beach bums can take their pick. This latter stretch, however, is the big daddy, running for two miles between the Harris highlands and a low peninsula with a bulbous tip. For further-flung beaches, take the Caledonian MacBrayne ferry (08705 650000, www.calmac.co.uk) from Leverburgh on Harris south to Berneray. There, mile after mile of undiscovered sand

beckons. North Uist, a neighbouring island linked to Berneray by a causeway, is similarly rich in scenery and sand. At all these beaches, you often have the place to yourself.

WHERE TO STAY AND EAT

The scenery at Luskentyre encourages wild camping. During the summer a collection of motor homes and tents pitch up on the grass to the north side of the bay.

The classiest hotel on the island is Scarista House (01859 550238, www.scarista house.com) by Traigh Scarista. A converted Georgian manse, it is small but beautiful. The restaurant does Franco-Scots cuisine using local ingredients and is open to non-residents.

Almost next door are the award-winning Blue Reef Cottages (01859 550370, www.stay-hebrides.com). Neolithic in inspiration and green by design, they have character and class, and are perfect for self-catering and stays of at least a week.

Down at the island's southern tip, by an old tumbledown harbour, the Rodel Hotel (01859 520210, www.rodelhotel.co.uk) offers clean and comfortable rooms and a sociable restaurant; hearty local seafood is a forte.

If touring South Harris and searching for a snack, the Skoon Art Café (01859 530268, www.skoon.com) does great soups, sandwiches and coffee. On the tiny 'golden road' up the south-east coast, it is off the beaten path; call for directions or follow the OS grid reference on its website. For all other pubs, B&Bs and facilities, head for Tarbert.

Luskentyre is a tiny hamlet, but the name generally refers to a trio of beaches: the eponymous strand, Rosamol and Seilebost.

HOW TO GET THERE

By car Travel to Skye, embark at Uig, then take the car ferry to Tarbert on Harris. Caledonian MacBrayne runs the crossing from Uig to Tarbert (1 hour 30 minutes), also the sailing from Ullapool to Stornoway on Lewis (2 hours 45 minutes), which is connected to Harris (01851 703773, 08705 650000, www.calmac.co.uk). **By bus** There are several buses a day on South Harris (Hebridean Transport, 01851 705050). These drop people on the A859 at the Luskentyre turn-off, then you have to walk. Rosamol is less than three miles away; other sands are far closer. **By air** Lewis and Harris actually form a single land mass, so it is possible to fly to Stornoway on Lewis, then go south to Luskentyre without recourse to ferries. Several airports provide regular services to Stornoway; the travel pages of the Western Isles Council (www.cne-siar.gov.uk) provide a good summary of carriers.

PARKING

Free parking. There is an informal car park in a cemetery at Rosamol, three miles beyond Luskentyre town. But you can park by the side of the road almost anywhere around here.

FACILITIES

Bins. Campsite. Caravan park. Slipway. Toilets (disabled).

SPORTS

Fishing. Sailing. Sea canoeing. Snorkelling. Surfing. Bring your own equipment (nearest hire centre is in Leverburgh on south side of Harris, Sound Watersports, 01859 520217).

SWIMMING

Safe for swimming, but watch out for the tow when the tide is ebbing. The average summer sea temperature is 12°C-13°C. No lifeguard or emergency facilities. Water quality: clean, but not MCS tested.

RULES

Barbecues, camping, dogs and fires are permitted.

FURTHER REFERENCE

Tourist information, Tarbert, Isle of Harris (April-October, 01859 502011, www. visithebrides.com). Local council (01851 703773, www.cne-siar.gov.uk).

Sandwood Bay

Postcards from the edge.

The beach at Sandwood Bay, cast away on the north-western tip of Scotland, is less than two miles long – but its legend is much, much bigger. Taking centre stage at the tideline, a couple of spooky rock formations form the backdrop for various mysterious goings-on. There have been several reported mermaid sightings; people also claim to have seen the ghost of a bearded sailor of Armada vintage hereabouts. At the beginning of 2005, Grampian Television even managed to persuade Brian Cox, the original screen Hannibal Lecter, to front a series on Scottish mysteries called *Beyond Explanation*. Sandwood, being Sandwood, merited an episode all to itself.

It may be haunted, but it is also haunting. Remote and implacable, Sandwood is a beach that is utterly indifferent to human presence. Marooned in a forgotten corner of Sutherland, overpowered by the massive skies and relentless sea, one suddenly understands the meaning of the word sublime, as the Romantic artists defined it.

When driving up to this lonely outpost, access to Sandwood Bay is via 'the last road on the left' – beyond Ullapool, beyond Assynt, beyond virtually everything. Your last glimpses of civilisation are at Kinlochbervie on Loch Inchard, a small fishing port with a population of less than 500. As you continue up the coast, there are a few dispersed crofting settlements – not so much villages as clusters of houses.

This has always been a sparsely populated, faraway place. In the nearby settlement of Inshegra, during the post-war period, classes at the schoolhouse – since converted into the Old School restaurant – were suspended when a car drove past, such was the excitement. Back then, seeing a private motor vehicle was a rare event. Today, this sense of separation and distance endures.

Indeed, there is no proper road to Sandwood Bay, just a four-mile track from the hamlet of Blairmore. The scenery en route can hardly be described as remarkable: a dark moorland dotted with minor lochans leading into a peat-bog emptiness. After three miles, however, you emerge round the shoulder of Druim na Buainn, a wee pudding of a hill, and get a tantalising glimpse of the final destination. Down to your right is the desolate Sandwood Loch. A ruined cottage, also reputed to be haunted, overlooks its waters.

As you wind down the last of the path to Sandwood, its bloody-minded magnificence takes hold. Unsheltered, facing the worst the North Atlantic can offer, punctuated by the eerie sea stack of Am Buachaille, this beach is truly soul stirring.

At Sandwood, on the edge of the world amid fearsome seas, ordinary mortals soon realise that their opinions are mere words on the wind. It puts people in their place, a place

Am Buachaille, an ancient sea stack, sets the otherworldly tone at Sandwood.

that is not quite as grand as they thought. But you don't need to project images of ghosts to create a sense of anxiety: the bay has a sufficiency of real dead people for that.

Back in December 1893, a small fishing boat was lost just off the coast, having misjudged the winter weather. Of its five crew, one was never found, two bodies were located nearby, while the skipper and his teenage son were found at Sandwood, clinging together above the tide line. It is supposed they survived the wreck, made it ashore, then died of exposure, beyond help. The four bodies were buried at Oldshoremore cemetery.

Further evidence of shipwrecks was noted in *Highways And Byways In The West Highlands*, the 1935 book by Seton Gordon, the Scottish naturalist. Before the 1828 construction of the Cape Wrath lighthouse, the coast was seemingly a magnet for wrecks, although there are no remains of vessels today.

Despite the forlorn atmosphere, it it possible to do Sandwood in sociable mood: a few friends and a night in a tent; long June evenings; beers and banter; rolling around in the sand. Though the currents are strong and potentially dangerous, and the water frigid, some people swim; others come to surf. All the same, it is equally possible to arrive on a weekday in high summer and find yourself on the beach with only three people, who appear and disappear as they walk round dunes and rocks. The mood becomes entirely different. You look at that spooky stack, Am Buachaille, eroding over millennia. You gaze at the pattern of the sands changing continuously, at the waves washing in to shore, at the unpeopled hills inland. Suddenly, you question your own presence. The ghost stories become comprehensible. And your carefree day at the beach turns into an existential journey. Leave the bucket and spade at home, but bring some gravitas.

OTHER BEACHES

Oldshoremore, south of Sandwood Bay, is a pint-sized dynamo. The turquoise waters and luxurious golden sands are framed by a barren, craggy landscape. In keeping with Sandwood's mysterious air, the beach is located beyond an old cemetery (tip: it's on the way from Kinlochbervie to the car park at Blairmore). Immediately round the headland to its north, the Polin beach is another tiny gem – a miniature version of Oldshoremore and Sandwood. To get there, you'll have to get back into the car (drive back round the road, via Oldshore Beg and Polin village, for access).

For other sands, head north-east to Durness. This remote crofting village sits on Sango Bay, where the beach blinds you with its brilliant blue and white palette. To the east, the beaches at Sangobeg and Ceannabeinne – untouched pearls framed by green hills – are even better. North-west of Durness is the great sweep of sand and dunes at Balnakeil Bay, beyond the eponymous craft village, a military base-turned-creative enclave.

WHERE TO STAY AND EAT

People do camp at Sandwood; it certainly saves the two-hour walk back to the car. And there's not much in the way of five-star accommodation around here. The Kinlochbervie Hotel (01971 521275, www.kinlochberviehotel.com) is an unremarkable 1970s-style building, but probably the closest hotel to the beach, with fine views of the fishing port.

The seasonal Old School at Inshegra (01971 521383, www.oldschoolklb.co.uk) is preferable for the standard of its bedrooms and scores big points for atmosphere in its dining room (once a Victorian school). The langoustine salad here is straight out of the water: simple and gorgeous.

The Rhiconich Hotel (01971 521224, www.rhiconichhotel.co.uk) is a basic roadside hotel set amid wild and rugged loch scenery. A fisherman's favourite, it is similarly suited to walkers and twitchers. The restaurant serves chicken korma, the usual roasts, and local specialities (haggis and cullen skink, a creamy fish soup). For B&B accommodation in the vicinity, see www.visithighlands.com.

Other alternatives are at Durness, up the A838. Mackays Rooms and Restaurant (01971 511202, www.visitmackays.com) offers tasteful bedrooms and ambitious cooking. A sample three-course offering includes wild boar with barbecue sauce; Arctic char with garlic, ginger and spring onion; fudge and mascarpone cheesecake.

The country kitchen-style Shorehouse (01971 502251, www.seafoodrestaurant-tarbet.co.uk), a seasonal restaurant at Tarbet, is worth the trip (take the A894 south of Laxford Bridge and a minor road west to Tarbet). They catch the fish themselves.

HOW TO GET THERE

By car From Ullapool, take the A835 then the A837, followed by the A894 to Laxford Bridge. Then take the A838 until you come to a junction at the hamlet of Rhiconich. Take the B801 for Kinlochbervie. Go through Kinlochbervie and keep on the minor road, past Oldshoremore, until you reach the settlement of Blairmore. At the car park, the footpath to Sandwood is clearly signposted. The beach is a 4.5-mile walk to the north. **By bus** The closest you can get is Kinlochbervie, seven miles away. In summer, a coach service runs once a day from Inverness (01349 883585, www.timdearman coaches.co.uk). **By train** A train from Inverness to Lairg (www.firstgroup.com/scotrail) links up with a limited local north-west bus service that also calls at Kinlochbervie (0871 200 2233, www.travelinescotland.com). **By air** The nearest airport is Inverness (01667 462445, www.hial.co.uk), which has regular flights to various UK destinations and car hire facilities.

PARKING

Free, *see above*.

FACILITIES

None.

SPORTS

Surfing, but bring your own board. Not recommended for novices.

SWIMMING

Exercise caution. No lifeguards. Strong currents. Water quality: clean (but not MCS rated).

RULES

Camping is permitted but not encouraged as this is a conservation area; take care when lighting fires. Dogs permitted, but must be kept on a lead as sheep roam free.

FURTHER REFERENCE

Tourist information, Durness, Sutherland (08452 255121, www.visithighlands. com). Local council (01463 702000, www.highland.gov.uk). Websites: www.mysteriousbritain.co.uk; www.undiscoveredscotland.co.uk.

Sinclair's Bay

Splendid isolation.

Travel writers often compare Sinclair's Bay to a Caribbean beach, owing to the pristine white sand, the dazzling blue seas and the desert island quality. That's on a sunny day. But with a cold North Sea pulsing against the shore, the north-east tip of Britain just a few miles away at Duncansby Head, and Norway just over the horizon, this is not exactly the stuff of *Beach Blanket Bingo*. Indeed, there is nothing here of the traditional seaside jaunt – no buckets, spades or sunscreen. Sitting on the edge of a distant and sparsely populated county, its beach lies more than 100 miles north of Inverness and can often be spookily devoid of life. Virtually no one comes here, bar the odd surfer when the swell comes in from the south-east, or the occasional millionaire seeking seclusion in Ackergill Tower, the cliff-top 15th-century castle. Plovers and dunlin outnumber people. No, Sinclair's Bay is large, empty, far away and utterly desolate. Yet it is a wonderful place for walking, talking and reflection.

Standing by the lighthouse at Noss Head, a lonely headland on the south side, you can take in the full sweep of the bay. The mouth is five miles across and the beach is a great three-mile arc of sand bisected by a small stream, with knuckled dunes backing on to Caithness, aka 'the Flow Country': miles and miles of low-lying peat bog and forest – a blank canvas for your imagination.

If nothing else, Sinclair's Bay offers space, a theatre for the mind. Local traffic passing up and down the A99 between Wick and John O'Groats, a few hundred yards inland, gives off a stunning sense of disregard, which can make a visitor on the shore feel frivolous. You could almost draw a collective speech bubble above the cars and vans saying, 'We have lives and businesses and things to do. You are standing on a strip of coastline that has nothing. Nothing. Why?'

In response, you might make a case for history – and architecture. The bay is named for the St Clair family who once held the Earldom of Caithness. A clan of high achievers, one of their number is said to have journeyed to Nova Scotia at the end of the 14th century. The St Clairs certainly built Rosslyn Chapel in Midlothian in the mid 15th century, recently brought to global prominence by *The Da Vinci Code*. The late 15th-century Castle Sinclair Girnigoe, now lying in ruins at the south end of Sinclair's Bay, was also their work. In fact, there are sometimes more castles here than people: the aforementioned Ackergill Tower sits right on the beach and, a mile north of the sands, the crumbling 16th-century Keiss Castle perches precariously on the cliff, with the 'new' 18th-century Keiss Castle nearby.

Indeed, the castles at Sinclair's Bay are positively modern given the history of the place. The very word Caithness derives from its Norse name of Katanes, 'headland of the

The old Keiss Castle,
one of four fortresses
along the beach.

Cat people', possibly referring to a local Pictish kingdom from the Dark Ages. Vikings were certainly coming here by the ninth or tenth centuries. Caithness is also dotted with brochs, defensive stone structures that date back some 2,000 years, and chambered cairns that are thought to be more than 5,000 years old. Estimates for the first post-Ice Age human settlement of the area are pegged about 7000 BC.

Walking on the beach, then, you have nine millennia of imaginary footprints to follow: from the original hunter-gatherers to Picts, from Vikings and St Clairs to modern tourists lost on their way to John O'Groats. At times, you half expect to stumble across some ancient, decrepit wooden chest with tarnished bronze seals, poking out of the sand.

Take away those historical musings, though, and Sinclair's Bay is a void, largely defined by absence – good for peace-seekers, philosophers and lone wolves, challenging for mainstream holidaymakers. There are no soaring mountains, no offshore islands to interrupt and enhance the horizon, and even the landmark sites – the lighthouse and castles – are so distant in most perspectives that they hardly register. Its beauty, however, lies in its simplicity.

The most striking feature, however, is often taken for granted. This far north, the sun rises in midsummer around 3am and doesn't set until 11pm. In fact, it hardly gets

properly dark at all, since the sun doesn't go very far beneath the horizon. The quality of light in the high months around June makes artists weep with happiness. And the distance from cities, coupled with cold nights, makes for glorious views of winter stars.

And yet, and yet: no one comes to Sinclair's Bay. There are no facilities, no dramatic scenery and nothing exciting going on. But still it makes the top ten beach lists. It seems that for some people, bleak beats the Caribbean any day.

OTHER BEACHES

Welcome to surf country. In this corner of the British Isles, enthusiasts in wetsuits brave the chilly waters at north coast beaches such as Thurso and Dunnet, just a short drive from Sinclair's Bay. Thurso Bay, also known as the gateway to the Orkneys, is a sometime venue for professional surf meets. Though the beach is right by the town, it offers wild and rugged views of Dunnet Head to the east. Dunnet beach, meanwhile, east of Thurso, comprises two majestic miles of sand backed by grassy dunes, with a lonely lighthouse – the northernmost on the British mainland – standing on Dunnet Head. Twitchers come a close second to surfers. They seek out red-throated divers, peregrines, black guillemot and rareties including waxwings and snow buntings. The best access is from the caravan and camping site towards the Dunnet village end.

For a different experience, try Freswick Bay, three miles south of John O'Groats, down a minor road off the A99. Bleak and abandoned, this secluded beach is overlooked by Freswick House, built by yet another local St Clair in the mid 18th century. Above, the sinister mansion is occupied by a filmmaker; with such a melancholy atmosphere, it is easy to see why. There are a couple of more ancient, atmospheric ruins a short way along the cliffs to the south, but watch your step – and your spirits.

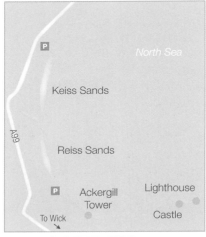

HOW TO GET THERE

By car Sinclair's Bay is about three miles north of Wick, which is 113 miles north of Inverness. The beach is split by a small stream with the northern half known as Keiss Beach, the more handsome southern stretch as Reiss Sands. Most visitors opt for the latter (down a minor road off the A99, signposted along with the adjacent golf course). For Keiss Beach, access from another minor road off the A99, by the hamlet of Keiss, seven miles north of Wick. **By train** Wick has a station although the train from Inverness takes four hours (www.firstgroup.com/scotrail). **By bus** Scottish Citylink runs a coach service from Inverness to Wick that takes about three hours (0870 550 5050, www.citylink.co.uk). Local bus services going to John O'Groats (01847 893123, www.rapsons.co.uk) can drop you on the main road. From there, it's less than a mile's walk to the beach. **By air** Wick has a small airport with flights from various UK destinations (www.hial.co.uk).

PARKING
Free parking next to the beach.

FACILITIES
None.

SPORTS
Golf (Wick Golf Club, 01955 602726, www.wickgolfclub.com).

SWIMMING
The waters are clean and cold (summer surface temperatures peak at 13°C). No lifeguard or emergency facilities. Water quality: not MCS tested.

RULES
No camping or fires. Dogs permitted.

FURTHER INFORMATION
John O'Groats tourist information (01955 611373). Local council (www.highland.gov.uk). Websites: www.visithighlands.com.

Even when the sun is shining, Sinclair's Bay is utterly deserted.

WHERE TO STAY AND EAT

Sinclair's Bay can seem bleak, but luxury is close at hand – if you can afford it. Overlooking the beach, the 15th-century Ackergill Tower (01955 603556, www.ackergill-tower.co.uk) has 25 lavish bedrooms and is available on a 'whole let' basis for 16 or more people, from prices of about £6,000 a day including everything except drinks. It is not a hotel – there is no reception, and no restaurant – but an elaborate private home. An array of themed weekend parties – food, shooting, Hogmanay – is also offered.

If that's beyond your budget, the Quayside (01955 603299, www.quayside wick.fsnet.co.uk) is an economical and friendly little B&B in nearby Wick, right at the harbour. Wick offers various other options, including the serviceable Mackays Hotel (01955 602323, www.mackayshotel.co.uk). Despite its professional gloss, it might be worth haggling over room prices here on a quiet night.

For the best food in the region, drive up to Scrabster (by Thurso) or south to Lybster. Scrabster boasts the harbourside Captain's Galley (01847 894999, www.captains galley.co.uk): though stark and simply furnished, this is a seriously good seafood venue with excellent ethical policy, while Lybster has the Portland Arms Hotel (01593 721721, www.portlandarms.co.uk). This mid-Victorian coaching inn, with its Library restaurant, is also good for accommodation, but has kept its food focus through a couple of ownership changes in recent years. For other eats, check out Wick or Thurso.

Lunan Bay

Romance and intrigue on the North Sea.

What does a sleepy beach in the north-east of Scotland have in common with Woody Allen? Not much, at first glance. With its strip of red sand, a few dunes, the rhythm of the North Sea, and a rock grotto at its north end, this is a gem of a beach, arguably the most handsome stretch of coastline in Angus – and seemingly the last place to conjure images of a New York comedian. But, bizarrely, the ruined castle on the cliff, and the story behind it, calls to mind the Manhattan miserablist.

In the 1990s, Allen caused a commotion when he divorced his wife and married his stepdaughter. In 16th-century Angus, another *affair de coeur* went pear-shaped when a local aristocrat got the hots for his wife's daughter. Back then, they didn't bother with attorneys and due process. The result was a fine old-fashioned siege instead. If you stand on the sands at Lunan Bay, look up at the fragile remains of Red Castle, and wonder why it ever descended to such a state of disrepair, now you know.

The castle – built with characteristic red sandstone, hence the name – dates to the late 12th century and was initially meant to ward off Vikings. By the 16th century, it was in the hands of the Beaton family, who made what they thought was a shrewd marriage with the mature Lady Elizabeth plighting her troth to local worthy James Grey of Dunninald. James soon decided that he preferred Lady Elizabeth's lovely daughter, Isobel, and all hell broke loose. He was thrown out of Red Castle, but came back team-handed and attacked it over two years, from 1579 to 1581. That effectively ruined the old place, and it has been rotting for centuries.

Today, it is hard to imagine crimes of passion and epic battles in this forgotten corner. For all the history of the district, the ancient Pictish sites, bonny glens leading up to the Grampian Mountains, personable small towns, and the gee-whizz attractions – championship golf at Carnoustie; the 12th-century abbey ruins at Arbroath – Angus is often overlooked by visitors to Scotland, even by Scots themselves. It lacks the urban delights of Edinburgh or Glasgow and the heightened visual drama of the Highlands and Islands. Aberdeen is right on its doorstep, but Angus still feels set aside, no longer an arena for hot-blooded emotions, brutality and romance. The population here tends to be older than the Scottish average and visitors are few and far between. This doubtless frustrates the local tourist industry, but can only benefit those looking for sands that are both accessible and quiet, like those at Lunan Bay.

After you have ruminated on 16th-century love and loss under the ruin's corroded silhouette, explore the strand. The bay is cut in half by Lunan Water, a stream that runs by Red Castle. At the very north end, the bay is briefly touched by the main east coast railway line. Some train passengers going the distance to Aberdeen can occasionally strike it lucky and look over their shoulder at just the right moment to see the sweep of the bay recede, a few minutes before Montrose. The line is fairly discreet, however, and hardly detracts from the aesthetics of the beach.

Once a hotbed of lust and violence, Lunan Bay is now a sleepy and unsung stretch of Angus coast.

Visual highlights at the north end include craggy sandstone rock formations, worn away by the waves, and at one point shaped into an abrupt grotto, a go-nowhere cave. You can walk through these rocks at low tide, but wouldn't want to be thrown against them by a rising swell: they are rough and uneven, pocked with shells and edges. On the foreshore, fishing nets are pegged in the sand, scooping up salmon and other riches brought in by the tide; on the beach, jewelled and stranded jellyfish glitter in the light; arms of land enclose the bay with a short embrace.

Surfers come here sometimes, and you might see the occasional local riding a horse along the beach, but even in high summer there are days when nothing seems to happen, and a venturesome family with picnic and wet wipes is as rowdy as it gets. When the sea is calm, the tide is so gentle is doesn't so much wash against the shore as insinuate itself.

Try as you might to imagine melodrama and mayhem, that typical Angus dormancy throws a discreet blanket over the plaintive cries of Lady Elizabeth, the sobs of her daughter and the martial soundtrack of siege. Much older echoes of Viking invaders are stilled to the point of silence.

All you hear at Lunan Bay is the low white noise of the sea, and the occasional gull. But that is precisely why you come.

OTHER BEACHES

The Angus coastline has a whiff of the traditional British seaside about it. Arbroath, in particular, boasts two miles of sands, a caravan site and acclaimed chippies back at the harbour; Montrose, further north, has several miles of open sand directly accessible from the town. Either are fine if you want the sand between your toes, and there is even more beach further south on the way to Dundee, in the strip of coast between Carnoustie and Broughty Ferry (closed at Buddon Ness because of nearby rifle ranges on Barry Links behind). But if you want wide sky and National Nature Reserve status, go further south still to Fife. Tentsmuir (www.nnr-scotland.org.uk) offers miles of sand backing on to an extensive pine forest, with excellent birdwatching. It's just over the bridge from Dundee.

WHERE TO STAY AND EAT

Combining proximity to the beach with characterful local architecture, Lunan Bay Accommodation (01241 830222, www.lunan-bay-accommodation.info) is a good bet. Available by the week, the self-catering houses hold six or eight people; a cute salmon fishing bothy is refurbished as a hideaway for two.

For an overnight stay, Gordon's (01241 830364, www.gordonsrestaurant.co.uk), at nearby Inverkeilor, holds great appeal. The three bedrooms are not the height of luxury, but this establishment has great credibility. The restaurant below is something of a local legend; the food, a Franco-Scots mélange, is the finest for miles around.

The most jaw-dropping B&B in the locale is Ethie Castle (01241 830434, www.ethiecastle.com), south-east of Inverkeilor. An awesome and authentic red sandstone fortress, it has a few stylish rooms – touches range from traditional four-poster beds to art deco bathrooms – and smart public rooms with log fires. Dinner is often served to residents in the Tudor kitchen by a log fire.

For hearty and uncomplicated cooking, go down the coast to Auchmithie. The But'n'Ben (01241 877223) should end all debate about what constitutes a Scottish restaurant; expect farmhouse kitchen-style cuisine with old-school puddings.

For other accommodation and food, head for Montrose or Arbroath (especially Marco's On The Shore and Peppo's, Arbroath's harbourfront fish and chip shops).

The fishing nets scoop up salmon and the shore is dotted with tidal jewels.

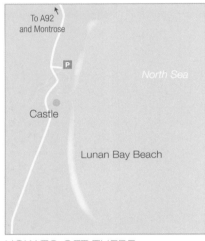

To A92
and Montrose

North Sea

Castle

Lunan Bay Beach

HOW TO GET THERE

By car Lunan Bay is north of Dundee between Arbroath and Montrose, off the A92, with access via the tiny hamlet of Lunan. **By train** The nearest railway stations are at Montrose and Arbroath (www.firstgroupcom/scotrail). **By bus** There are frequent local bus services between Arbroath and Montrose, although they will drop you more than a mile short of the beach (check with Abroath Tourist Information Centre or on the transport pages of the local authority website; for both *see below*). The minor roads just inland from this stretch of coast form part of the National Cycle Network, which goes through Lunan (www.sustrans.org.uk).

PARKING

Free parking next to the beach.

FACILITIES

Rubbish bins (including dog waste bins).

SPORTS

Canoeing (www.canoescotland.com). Fishing (01573 470612, www.fiskesks.co.uk).

SWIMMING

The beach is fine for swimming, but the summer sea surface temperature peaks at 13°C-14°C. No lifeguard or emergency facilities. Water quality: MCS recommended.

RULES

No bonfires or camping. Dogs are permitted.

FURTHER REFERENCE

Arbroath Tourist Information Centre (01241 872609). Dundee Tourist Information Centre (01674 673232, www.angusanddundee.co.uk). Local council (08452 777778, www.angus.gov.uk).

The ruins of Red Castle bring a sense of romance to the beach.

Seacliff

Between a rock and an old place.

The Bass Rock is just one talking point at Seacliff beach. A great guano-encrusted volcanic hump, covered in gannets, it dominates the horizon. Breaching the water by 350 feet, a mile out to sea, it resembles a truncated take-off ramp; from a different vantage point, it could be a cartoon whale. As a backdrop to tales of mystery and derring-do, it has served Scottish authors all the way from Robert Louis Stevenson (*Catriona*, 1893) to James Robertson (*The Fanatic*, 2000). As a background to photographs, it is a snapper's best friend. Back on the mainland, sitting romantically on top of the bluffs, the magnificent ruins of Tantallon Castle are Seacliff's other showpiece. Dating back to the 14th century, this red sandstone pile breathed its last under Cromwell's artillery in 1651. At the west end of Seacliff, both these features of the landscape – natural and cultural – loom large. Sand, safe waters, rock pools, woodland and visual variety complete the package for Edinburgh's discerning day trippers, and those who come from further afield.

East Lothian does not lack for beaches, but Seacliff stands out from the crowd. Since it is east of North Berwick, Edinburghians consider it off the beaten path and many steer clear. It also completely lacks facilities, which further deters the mainstream – anyone who wants an ice-cream van and pub, or those seeking formal distractions for the kids.

Seacliff is more a low-key, laid-back beach. The kind of place where you would see a sea kayak being untethered from the car roof, preternaturally happy retired couples venting creatively by building sandcastles and moats of Byzantine complexity, or evidence of odd little Goldsworthy-style sculptures, mini-henges to be washed away by tide and elements. It still has the shouting children, of course, groups of youth, and beautiful people playing desultory games of beach tennis, but somehow it all seems quite discreet. And, despite the lack of candyfloss, it's hard to get bored here.

That anomalous white rock offshore is just one focus of interest; the Isle of May, further out in the Forth, another. It is those red walls of Tantallon Castle, though, that add romance. Legend has it that when Cromwell invaded Scotland, 100 guerrilla fighters held the castle for a fortnight against a besieging force of more than 3,000 men and artillery.

Tantallon and the Bass Rock may dominate the western skyline, but Seacliff has a hidden string to its bow: one of Scotland's tiniest harbours. Tucked away beneath the Gegan, the beach's western headland, it cannot be seen from ground level. But climb the rocks at the end of the beach and the deep, compact enclosure presents itself. Chiselled from the surrounding sandstone, it was built in the late Victorian period, a haven for small fishing boats. It now often serves as an informal summer plunge pool for boys shucking off some adolescent energy. Elsewhere at that end of Seacliff, root around in the rocks.

The beach itself is a short crescent – a few hundred yards of pinky-gold sand, hemmed in by low, dense woodland. Because of its limited size, it might not be ideal for long, windswept winter walks. But on warm summer day, when nearby North Berwick is chock-a-block with day trippers, crowded tea rooms and cars, Seacliff is a respite. It is popular, of course, but only to the point of being sociable rather than seriously crowded.

If the west end of the beach is synonymous with castle and rock, the east end's defining symbol is a majestic cross that seemingly rises out of the sea. On a long finger of reef, jutting into the Forth, the simple stone pillar and cross are called St Baldred's Beacon. Baldred was an eighth-century holy man of this parish whose CV included

The tiny Victorian harbour, and Tantallon Castle beyond, are a couple of the beach's talking points.

'extensive experience of the hermit life'. The lone wolf retreated to a chapel (now ruined) out on the Bass Rock – just him, the gannets, and God.

History is in the air here, and the soil. In the vicinity of the beach, there are also the tumbledown and overgrown ruins of the 16th-century Auldhame Castle, and the shell of Seacliff House, destroyed by fire in 1907.

When sitting on the shoreline, however, you don't have to spend all – or any – of your time thinking about Dark Age hermits, Cromwellian sieges, archaeology or Scottish literature. You can just gaze absently out to sea, looking north to Fife (about 12 miles away) or north-east towards nothing at all. Then a flash of white might catch your eye, gannets from the Bass Rock fishing, hovering high in the air, waiting, waiting, then dropping impossibly fast and deep into the water, streamlined thieves from another element who struck their own ancient deal with gravity. They may have aided Baldred's contemplation around 1,300 years ago, or Robert Louis Stevenson's muse rather more recently. Some passing afternoon at Seacliff, they might even do something for you.

OTHER BEACHES

The coast east of Edinburgh is one long string of beaches. The first one is the city's own Portobello, characterised by amusements, a promenade and a sense of faded glory. The first one worth seeking out, however, is further east. The long strand at Longniddry Bents leads to Gosford Sands, and the nature reserve at Aberlady Bay – a marvellous, desolate beach with views of Arthur's Seat and wrecked World War II submarines poking out of the sand. In the autumn, thousands of pink-footed geese descend on Aberlady. As you'd expect, this whole atmospheric stretch is more for walks and talks than sunbathing.

Next up, heading east, is the smart village of Gullane, which possesses an excellent curvaceous mile of sands. When you walk east, it leads to a series of smaller beaches and inlets. Yellowcraigs, further along, has nature trails and a barbecue area, while North Berwick itself has a very popular town beach, running just east of its harbour, with views of yachts and the Bass Rock, but from the other side.

HOW TO GET THERE

By car Seacliff is 28 miles east of Edinburgh. Take the A1 from Edinburgh to Tranent and then take the A198 and follow the coast past North Berwick. Alternatively, follow the A1 to East Linton and take the A198 north to Auldhame. Access is via the private road through Auldhame Farm; cyclists and pedestrians go free, drivers have to pay £2 to pass an automated barrier (no change available or given so remember to bring two £1 coins). The final approach to the beach is a rough track. **By train** North Berwick is the nearest rail station. **By bus** North Berwick is well served by regular buses (0870 608 2608, www.firstgroup.com) and trains from Edinburgh, but there is no public transport beyond that.

PARKING

Pay parking.

FACILITIES

None. North Berwick is the nearest spot for public toilets and shops.

SPORTS

Canoeing. Diving (Edinburgh Diving Centre, 0131 229 4838, www.edinburgh diving.co.uk). Kayaking. Rafting (Craigmillar Adventure Project, 0131 652 1557, www.capro.org.uk). Sailing (South Gyle Royal Yachting Association Scotland, 0131 317 7388, www. rya.org.uk). Surfing.

SWIMMING

Safe to swim but no lifeguard or emergency facilities. Water quality: MCS recommended.

RULES

No fires or barbecues. Dogs permitted on beach. Visitors discouraged after sunset.

FURTHER REFERENCE

Tourist information, North Berwick (01506 832121, www.edinburgh.org). Local council (01620 827827, www.east lothian.gov.uk). Websites: www. visitscotland.com; www.undiscovered scotland.co.uk.

The Bass Rock dominates the horizon at the western end of Seacliff beach.

Beyond Seacliff, to the south-east, there is the gorgeous surprise package of the Peffer-Ravensheugh Sands, then the expanse of Tyne Sands and Belhaven Bay, all of these in John Muir Country Park (www.eastlothian.gov.uk). Facing directly out to the North Sea, these can be wilder than the more sheltered Forth beaches, and better for surfing.

WHERE TO STAY AND EAT

North Berwick has the biggest selection of eating and drinking options. The Macdonald Marine Hotel and Spa (0870 830 4812, www.macdonaldhotels.co.uk) may be part of a chain, but it is an authentic Victorian building, lately refurbished, with a decent spa.

Greywalls at Gullane (01620 842144, www.greywalls.co.uk) is the class of the local field. Of Edwardian vintage, it was built by Edward Lutyens and is cheek-by-jowl with the championship golf course at Muirfield. The formal dining room has a classy menu that makes use of prime logal ingredients: Aberdeen Angus steaks and Shetland salmon. La Potinière (01620 843214, www.la-potiniere.co.uk), also in Gullane, is a small and long-established Franco-Scots classic.

Over in Haddington, Bonars (01620 822100) serves Modern British cuisine in an old mill, while the perennial favourite Waterside bar-bistro (01620 825674) sits by a famous bridge over the Tyne. On a fine day, for tea with a view, head for the Scottish Seabird Centre at North Berwick (01620 890202, www.seabird.org) and sit on the terrace.

For other options, try Dirleton, Aberlady or Edinburgh.

Further reference

For additional websites relating to a specific area,
see the information box at the end of each chapter.

BEACHES/COAST

Adopt a Beach, www.adoptabeach.org.uk
BBC Coast, www.bbc.co.uk/coast
Beachcombing, www.glaucus.org.uk/hightide.htm
Beach hut rentals & sales, www.beach-huts.com
Blue Flag Beaches, www.blueflag.org
BritishCoast.Net, www.britishcoast.net
British National Sandcastle Building Competition,
   Great Yarmouth, www.great-yarmouth.co.uk
Cornwall Beach Guide, www.cornwall-beaches.co.uk
Devon Beach Guide, www.devonguide.com/beaches
Good Beach Guide, www.goodbeachguide.co.uk
Marine Conservation Society, www.mcsuk.org
Quality Coast, www.qualitycoast.org
Seawatch Foundation,
   www.seawatchfoundation.org.uk
UK Marine Special Areas of Conservation,
   www.ukmarinesac.org.uk
UNESCO Dorset and East Devon Coast,
   www.jurassiccoast.com
UK Fossil Collecting Locations, www.ukfossils.co.uk

BUS

National Express, www.nationalexpress.co.uk

CAMPING

Camping & Caravanning Club,
   www.campingandcaravanningclub.co.uk
Camping, Caravan & Touring Holiday Directory,
   www.campinguk.com
Scottish Camping & Caravanning,
   www.scottishcamping.com
UK Caravan & Campsite Directory,
   www.ukcampsite.co.uk/sites

CYCLING

Bike For All, www.bikeforall.net
Byways & Bridleways Trust, www.bbtrust.org.uk
British Cycling, www.britishcycling.org.uk
Cycle Touring & Countryside North Wales,
   www.conwyctc.fsnet.co.uk
International Mountain Biking Association,
   www.imba.com
National Cycle Network, www.ctc.org.uk
Tandem Club, www.tandem-club.org.uk
Trail Cyclist Association, www.trailquest.co.uk
Sustrans, www.sustrans.org.uk
Wheels for All, http://cpnw.newcomweb.demon.com

DISABLED

Bike for All, www.bikeforall.net
DisAbility Holidays.net, www.disabilityholidays.net
Holiday Care Services, www.holidaycare.org.uk
Tourism for All, www.tourismforall.org.uk
Wheelchair Travel & Access Minibuses,
   www.wheelchair-travel.co.uk
Wheels for All, http://cpnw.newcomweb.demon.com

ENVIRONMENTAL & CONSERVATION ORGANISATIONS

Association for the Protection of Rural Scotland,
   www.ruralscotland.org
British Association of Nature Conservationists,
   www.banc.org.uk
British Marine Life Study Centre,
   www.glaucus.org.uk
Campaign for the Protection of Rural England,
   www.cpre.org.uk
Campaign for the Protection of Rural Wales,
   www.cprw.org.uk
Carbon Footprint, www.carbonfootprint.com
Environment Agency,
   www.environment-agency.gov.uk
Environmental Protection UK, www.nsca.org.uk
Friends of the Earth, www.foe.co.uk
Greenpeace, www.greenpeace.org.uk
Marine Biodiversity and Ecosystem Functioning,
   www.marbef.org
**Marine Life Information Network for Britain and
   Ireland**, www.marlin.ac.uk
Natural England, www.naturalengland.org.uk
Sea Trust, www.seatrust.org.uk
Surfers Against Sewage,
   http://surfersagainstsewage.co.uk
World Wide Fund for Nature, www.wwf.org.uk

FISHING

Anglersnet, www.anglersnet.co.uk
Environment Agency Fishing Regulations,
   www.environment-agency.gov.uk/subjects/fish/
Fishing in Scotland, http://fish.visitscotland.com
Fishing Wales, www.fishing.visitwales.com
National Federation of Sea Anglers, www.nfsa.org.uk
Total Fishing, www.total-fishing.com

HERITAGE ORGANISATIONS

Cadw (the official guardian of the built heritage of
   Wales), www.cadw.wales.gov.uk
English Heritage, www.english-heritage.org.uk
International Council on Monuments & Sites UK,
   http://icomos-uk.org
National Trust, www.nationaltrust.org.uk
National Trust for Scotland, www.nts.org.uk
Scottish National Heritage, www.snh.org.uk
UK World Heritage Sites, www.ukworldheritage.org.uk
UNESCO, www.unesco.org

HORSE RIDING

British Horse Society, www.bhs.org.uk
Byways & Bridleways Trust, www.bbtrust.org.uk

NATURISM

Bare Britain, www.barebritain.com
British Naturism, www.british-naturism.org.uk/beaches
Naturist UK Fact File, http://nuff.org.uk

SAFETY

British Activity Holiday Association or Safe Quality Activity Holidays, www.baha.org.uk
Marine & Coastguard Association, www.mcga.gov.uk
National Water Safety Forum, www.nationalbeachsafety.org.uk
Royal Life Saving Society UK, www.lifesavers.org.uk
Royal National Lifeboat Institute, www.rnli.org.uk
Surf Life Saving GB, www.surflifesaving.org.uk

SPORTS

British Beach Volleyball, www.beach-volleyball.co.uk
British Federation of Sand and Land Yacht Clubs, www.bfslyc.org.uk
British Hang Gliding and Paragliding Association, www.bhpa.co.uk
British Kitesurfing Association, www.kitesurfing.org
British Waterski Online, www.britishwaterski.org.uk
British Waveski Association, www.waveski.co.uk
British Sub Aqua Club, www.bsac.com
British Sub Aqua Club Snorkelling, www.bsacsnorkelling.co.uk
Canoe&KayakUK, www.canoekayak.co.uk
England Beach Handball, www.beachhandball.org.uk
England's Golf Coast, www.englandsgolfcoast.com
Kayak Britain, www.kayakbritain.co.uk
Royal Yachting Association, www.rya.org.uk
Scottish Sport, www.scottishsport.co.uk
Sea Kayaking, www.seakayakinguk.com
Surf Kayaking Great Britain, www.bcusurf.org.uk
Sussex Hang Gliding and Paragliding, www.sussexhgpg.co.uk.
UKClimbing.com, www.ukclimbing.com
UK Windsurfing Association, http://ukwindsurfing.com

SWIMMING

British Long Distance Swimming Association, www.bldsa.org.uk
Lidos in the UK (including tidal saltwater pools), www.lidos.org.uk
Swim Trek Adventure Holidays, www.swimtrek.com

SURFING

A1 Surf, www.a1surf.com
British Surfing Association, www.britsurf.co.uk
National Surfing Centre, www.nationalsurfingcentre.com
Surfing England, www.surfingwaves.com/travel/england.htm

TOURISM

EnjoyEngland, www.enjoyengland.com
Visit Britain, www.visitbritain.com
Visit Scotland, www.visitscotland.com
Visit Wales, www.visitwales.com

TRANSPORT PLANNING

AA Route Planner, www.theaa.com/travelwatch
BBC Travel News, www.bbc.co.uk/travelnews
Traveline (public transport information), www.traveline.org.uk

TRAIN BOOKING INFORMATION

National Rail Enquiries, 08457 484950, www.nationalrail.co.uk
Train Line, www.thetrainline.com

WALKING

British Orienteering, www.britishorienteering.org.uk
Go4awalk.com, www.go4awalk.com
Hillwalking.org.uk, www.hillwalking.org.uk
Long Distance Walkers Association, www.ldwa.org.uk
National Trail, www.nationaltrail.co.uk
Ramblers Association, www.ramblers.org.uk
Scottish Orienteering, www.scottish-orienteering.org
South West Coastal Path, www.southwestcoastpath.com
Walking Englishman, www.walkingenglishman.com
Walklink.com, www.walklink.com
Walking-Routes.co.uk, www.walking-routes.co.uk

WILDLIFE

Badger Trust, www.badger.org.uk
Bat Conservation Trust, www.bats.org.uk
Botanical Society of the British Isles, www.bsbi.org.uk
British Dragonfly Society, www.dragonflysoc.org.uk
British Trust for Ornithology, www.bto.org.uk
Butterfly Conservation, www.butterfly-conservation.org
Dolphin Care, www.dolphincareuk.org
Mammal Society, www.abdn.ac.uk/mammal
RSPB, www.rspb.org.uk
RSPCA, www.rspca.org.uk
Seabird Group, www.seabirdgroup.org.uk
Sea Bird Colonies Scotland, www.ntsseabirds.org.uk
Save Our Seals, www.saveourseals.co.uk
Scotland's National Nature Reserves, www.nnr-scotland.org.uk
Scottish National Heritage, www.snh.org.uk
Scottish Wildlife Trust, www.swt.org.uk
Seal Sanctuary UK, www.sealsanctuary.co.uk
Shark Trust UK, www.sharktrust.org
Whale & Dolphin Conservation Society, www.wdcs.org
Wildfowl and Wetland Trust, www.wwt.org.uk
Wildlife Trusts, www.wildlifetrusts.org

YOUTH HOSTELS

Scottish Youth Hostels Association, www.syha.org.uk
UK Youth Hostels Association, www.yha.org.uk

Where to go for…

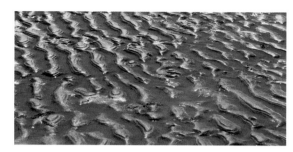

The Beaches